SpringerBriefs in Political Science

SpringerBriefs present concise summaries of cutting-edge research and practical applications across a wide spectrum of fields. Featuring compact volumes of 50 to 125 pages, the series covers a range of content from professional to academic. Typical topics might include:

- A timely report of state-of-the art analytical techniques
- A bridge between new research results, as published in journal articles, and a contextual literature review
- A snapshot of a hot or emerging topic
- An in-depth case study or clinical example
- A presentation of core concepts that students must understand in order to make independent contributions

SpringerBriefs in Political Science showcase emerging theory, empirical research, and practical application in political science, policy studies, political economy, public administration, political philosophy, international relations, and related fields, from a global author community.

SpringerBriefs are characterized by fast, global electronic dissemination, standard publishing contracts, standardized manuscript preparation and formatting guidelines, and expedited production schedules.

Dolors Palau-Sampio • Guillermo López-García

News, Media, and Communication in a Polarized World

A Spanish perspective

Dolors Palau-Sampio
Languages Theory and Communication Sciences
University of Valencia
Valencia, Spain

Guillermo López-García
Languages Theory and Communication Sciences
University of Valencia
Valencia, Spain

ISSN 2191-5466　　　　　ISSN 2191-5474　(electronic)
SpringerBriefs in Political Science
ISBN 978-3-031-86619-7　　　ISBN 978-3-031-86620-3　(eBook)
https://doi.org/10.1007/978-3-031-86620-3

This work was supported by Universitat de València (CIAICO/2021/125)

© The Editor(s) (if applicable) and The Author(s) 2025. This book is an open access publication.

Open Access This book is licensed under the terms of the Creative Commons Attribution 4.0 International License (http://creativecommons.org/licenses/by/4.0/), which permits use, sharing, adaptation, distribution and reproduction in any medium or format, as long as you give appropriate credit to the original author(s) and the source, provide a link to the Creative Commons license and indicate if changes were made.
The images or other third party material in this book are included in the book's Creative Commons license, unless indicated otherwise in a credit line to the material. If material is not included in the book's Creative Commons license and your intended use is not permitted by statutory regulation or exceeds the permitted use, you will need to obtain permission directly from the copyright holder.
The use of general descriptive names, registered names, trademarks, service marks, etc. in this publication does not imply, even in the absence of a specific statement, that such names are exempt from the relevant protective laws and regulations and therefore free for general use.
The publisher, the authors and the editors are safe to assume that the advice and information in this book are believed to be true and accurate at the date of publication. Neither the publisher nor the authors or the editors give a warranty, expressed or implied, with respect to the material contained herein or for any errors or omissions that may have been made. The publisher remains neutral with regard to jurisdictional claims in published maps and institutional affiliations.

This Springer imprint is published by the registered company Springer Nature Switzerland AG
The registered company address is: Gewerbestrasse 11, 6330 Cham, Switzerland

If disposing of this product, please recycle the paper.

Acknowledgement

This book has been funded by the R+D+I project "Desconcierto informativo: Calidad precarizada, sobre(des)información y polarización" (CIAICO2021/125), granted by the Generalitat Valenciana.

Contents

1 **Introduction**... 1
   1.1 Changes in the Post-media Sphere........................... 3

2 **The New Communication Ecosystem** 7
   2.1 How Communication Has Changed: The Impact
       of Digitalisation.. 7
   2.2 Old and New Media: The Hybrid Communication Model 9
   2.3 New Actors and Audiences 10
   2.4 The Ambivalence of Mediatisation 12

3 **Fragmentation and Dissolution of the Public Sphere** 15
   3.1 The Public Space and Public Sphere....................... 15
   3.2 The Mediasphere: The Public Media Sphere................. 17
   3.3 The Post-media Public Sphere............................ 19

4 **Challenges in a Hostile Scenario** 23
   4.1 Ideological and Emotional Distancing, Belonging,
       and Exclusion.. 24
       4.1.1 Polarisation 24
       4.1.2 Populism 27
       4.1.3 Testing Populism and Polarisation.................. 29
   4.2 Disinformation... 36
       4.2.1 Perception of Disinformation in Spain 38

5 **Information Consumption and Trust** 51
   5.1 Credibility Crisis and Access to News..................... 52
   5.2 Degree of Information and Preferences..................... 53
       5.2.1 Proximity Information 54
       5.2.2 Relevant Topics 55
       5.2.3 Media Type 56
   5.3 Politicisation and Exposure 60

6	**Quality of Information and Democracy**	63
	6.1 Definition and Identification	64
	6.2 Perception of Journalistic Quality	66
	6.2.1 The Journalists' Perspective	67
	6.2.2 Audience Assessment	67
	6.3 How Should Quality Improve?	72
7	**Disruption in the Information Industry: Precariousness and Professional "Decapitalisation"**	77
	7.1 The Media's Multifaceted Crisis	77
	7.2 Business Models and Their Alternatives	80
	7.3 Changes in Structure and Values	82
	7.4 Precarious Work and Its Manifestations	83
	7.5 Experiences in the Spanish Context	84
8	**Conclusions**	89
	References	95

List of Figures

Fig. 4.1 Bipartisanship in Spain: Percentage of votes for the two main political parties, 1977–2023. Source: prepared by the authors 26

Fig. 4.2 Comparison between the use of social networks and messaging apps and the detection of disinformation by age group (%) 46

List of Tables

Table 4.1	Degree of agreement or disagreement with the following statements (%)	29
Table 4.2	Degree of importance of disinformation in Spain (%)	39
Table 4.3	Contribution of the Internet and social networks to disinformation (%)	40
Table 4.4	Sources of disinformation (%)	40
Table 4.5	Degree of disinformation originating in different areas (%)	42
Table 4.6	Should public authorities take action against disinformation? (%)	43
Table 4.7	Preferred actions against disinformation (%)	44
Table 4.8	Detection of disinformation on social media or messaging apps (%)	45
Table 4.9	Comparison between consumption and identified disinformation (%)	45
Table 4.10	On which social networks or messaging apps have you detected disinformation? By gender and ideology (%)	47
Table 4.11	Reaction to detection of fake news on social media or messaging apps (%)	48
Table 4.12	Reactions to content you like or dislike on social media (%)	49
Table 4.13	Actions taken before sharing content (%)	50
Table 5.1	Most preferred information topics (%)	54
Table 5.2	Topics of most interest to stay informed (%)	55
Table 5.3	Comparison between media used (%)	57
Table 5.4	Media commonly used to obtain information (%)	59
Table 5.5	Ideological positioning of media outlets (scale 1 to 10)	61
Table 6.1	Perception of media quality in Spain (%)	68
Table 6.2	Perception of the evolution of media quality in Spain (%)	68
Table 6.3	Aspects that most contribute to reducing quality (%)	70
Table 6.4	Content types most often associated with quality problems (%)	71

Table 6.5	Media that best guarantee quality, according to management and scope of coverage (%)	72
Table 6.6	Ways to improve quality (%)	74
Table 6.7	Who should Be responsible for ensuring media quality? (%)	75

Chapter 1
Introduction

Communication is a fundamental aspect of the human condition, inherently containing a social component that connects humans to one another. From this premise, analysing communication in any of its dimensions, particularly within the public sphere, requires the historical, socio-political, technological, and economic contexts in which they occur to be identified and acknowledged. Aware of the need to adopt multiple perspectives to comprehend the rapid transformations, the authors of this book offer a complex approach that allows readers to take the pulse of the communication ecosystem that has emerged in the first quarter of the twenty-first century.

This ecosystem reflects a crossroads where numerous actors and factors converge and interact, with new digital technologies playing a fundamental role, bringing significant consequences for democratic coexistence. From a global perspective on the changes experienced by democracies worldwide, this work focuses on and examines them from a Spanish viewpoint.

News, Media, and Communication in a Polarised World. A Spanish Perspective combines theoretical and empirical approaches to analyse and contextualise the changes that the communication ecosystems, particularly the media, have undergone. The book is an attempt to address the confusion characterising an era of information overabundance—where infinite sources theoretically guarantee enrichment and diversity in the public sphere—while also dealing with the era of post-truth, where misinformation becomes a threat that fuels polarisation and populism.

In this context, traditional actors in the provision of information, namely the media, are also facing a situation of vulnerability caused by a multifaceted crisis. At a time when circumstances would demand greater strength, unquestionable quality, and an image of rigour and trust, the current state of the media reveals a very different picture. Weakened by the influence of platforms and social networks, plagued by serious economic difficulties, and questioned by audiences, their future role remains an unresolved mystery. Far from being irrelevant, the role that traditional media has played over the past century—as shapers of the public sphere and as a necessary safeguard of democracy—requires careful examination of their transformation.

This book is the culmination of a research project entitled "Informational bewilderment: Precarious quality, over(dis)information and polarisation" (CIAICO2021/125), carried out by the Mediaflows (www.mediaflows.es/en) research group and funded by the Generalitat Valenciana. It incorporates the findings of several research studies, developed using both quantitative and qualitative methodologies, such as a survey of 1200 people across Spain and focus groups with junior and senior journalists.

The combination of research methods enriches the analysis of the subject matter. In this case, one of the quantitative methods used—the survey, which enables systematic, anonymous, and representative questioning of a broad population—is complemented by focus groups, where the experiences and personal insights of journalists provide valuable depth and reveal important nuances.

The online survey, which took an average of 14 min to complete, was conducted throughout Spain from 8 to 15 March 2023. This timing was selected to evaluate the key issues 2 months before the municipal and regional elections (excluding Catalonia, the Basque Country, Andalusia, Galicia, and Castilla y León), in a year when a general election was also scheduled, which was later brought forward to July.

The questionnaire, consisting of 48 questions, was divided into three sections: information consumption (what type of content and through which channels it is consumed), perception of the quality of information and evaluation of disinformation (opinions on the quality of the media in Spain and assessments of the current situation), and evaluation of disinformation. The questionnaire design included dichotomous and multiple-choice responses, open-ended responses, and Likert scale models to assess the levels of agreement or disagreement with given statements (Bertram 2008).

The 1200 questionnaires were completed by respondents aged 16 or older. The margin of error for the total sample was +2.83, with $P = Q = 50\%$, under the assumption of maximum indeterminacy. The sample distribution was proportional to the population of each autonomous community and also took into account variables such as gender, age, and where respondents lived. Accordingly, 52% of responses came from women and 48% from men. Six age brackets representative of the population pyramid were considered: 16–24 (11.1%), 25–34 (12.7%), 35–44 (16.8%), 45–54 (19.0%), 55–64 (16.4%), and over 65 (23.9%). The responses also reflected population distribution across different habitats: fewer than 10,000 inhabitants (20.2%), between 10,001 and 50,000 (26.7%), between 50,001 and 200,000 (22.8%), between 200,001 and 500,000 (13.9%), and more than 500,000 (16.4%). In addition, the survey included variables such as population size, level of education, views on religion, and political self-positioning.

The focus groups with junior and senior journalists, lasting between 120 and 150 min, were conducted in person in March 2024 at the head office of the market research, analysis, and data company, Gfk, in Valencia. In addition to considering generational perspectives, the design of both focus groups aimed to achieve gender balance and representation of diverse media outlets (radio, press, television, news agencies, and communications departments). The senior journalists' focus group (those over 40 years old) included five women and three men, while the junior journalists' focus group (under 35 years old) included five men and three women.

In a moderated session, journalists discussed five general topics: the current situation and the current state of the profession and its evolution in recent years; comparisons of training and career prospects across generations; the impact of successive crises on employment and precariousness; mental health, work-life balance issues, and the shift towards institutional journalism; and professional independence, journalistic quality, and the relationship with audiences.

1.1 Changes in the Post-media Sphere

The book *News, Media, and Communication in a Polarised World. A Spanish Perspective* comprises eight chapters that analyse the principal changes in the so-called post-media public sphere, three decades after the integration of the media into the Internet.

After the Introduction chapter, *The New Communication Ecosystem* begins with a reflection on McLuhan's visionary insights into the omnipresence of media in everyday life, as formulated six decades ago in Understanding Media (1964), and extends these ideas to the present day. Alongside an observation of how the digital dimension and its characteristics have reinforced this phenomenon through the integration of previous media logics, this section explores the hybridisation processes that facilitate the coexistence of old and new media and the role of audiences within this context.

As highlighted in the opening chapter, these various transformations have given rise to a changing and confusing communication ecosystem, which involves a redefinition of the centrality of the media and its traditional role in favour of a growing prominence of social networks. Throughout its pages, different perspectives are explored within a complex scenario, where the ability to select, the fragmentation of audiences, and generational factors hold significant weight. From the paradox of a media landscape where the role of traditional media is declining and losing centrality (Bennett and Iyengar 2008), this section discusses its effective role in the mediation process.

The third chapter, *Fragmentation and Dissolution of the Public Sphere*, revisits the changes in the communication system to analyse how these transformations affect the process of shaping public opinion. After re-examining the concepts of public space and public sphere, this section focuses on the characteristics of the so-called mediasphere, the public sphere agreed upon by and within the mass media. It then discusses how the changes experienced in recent decades, following the introduction of digital technologies, have contributed to the definition of the post-media public sphere (López-García and Valera-Ordaz 2024), where public space has expanded and fragmented.

This section highlights the contradictory consequences of a process in which informational pluralism and the multiplicity of messages, rather than fostering a large public space that encourages exchange and the search for consensus, have led to the creation of multiple public spaces and greater polarisation. The causes that have blurred Habermas' concept of an inclusive public sphere of debate and consensus (Habermas 1997) are analysed, illustrating how these changes have led to an increase in noise, the dispersion of voices, and fragmentation, alongside a shortage of references. Echo chambers have further entrenched comfort spaces, fuelled by ideological biases (Llorca-Abad and Gamir-Ríos 2023).

Lastly, this section explores Habermas' (2023) reflections on the democratic and deliberative potential of new digital communication platforms, which is limited by the persistence of economic interests and the often superficial, partisan, and demagogic uses of these platforms.

Under the title of *Challenges in a Hostile Scenario,* the fourth chapter addresses the socio-political conditions in which communication occurs, delving into the perverse synergies between three major threats facing Western democracies: polarisation, disinformation, and the rise of populism (Svolik 2019; Tenove 2020; Schia and Gjesvik 2020; McKay and Tenove 2021; Schünemann 2022). This section combines a theoretical and empirical approach to the three concepts on which it pivots, based on a bibliographic review and a survey that takes the pulse and delves into the perception of citizens.

The first part of the chapter focuses on the dynamics of populism and polarisation, considering socio-political trends in the international context and how they manifest within the Spanish context. Through the survey, both dimensions have been tested based on the positioning of citizens in response to a series of statements. These responses allow us to observe both social fractures and support for certain populist attitudes concerning representatives of various powers, including the political class, financial sectors, the media, and international organisations. The responses of 1200 individuals, representative of Spanish society, also allow us to identify the main fault lines around significant social issues such as national identity, gender equality, immigration, climate change, and housing.

The second part of the chapter looks at disinformation, offering a detailed analysis of this phenomenon within the Spanish context. Based on public responses, an overview is provided of how citizens perceive the problem of disinformation, the sources they attribute to the origin of false content, how they act when such content is detected, and what measures receive public support in combating it. The results provide a comprehensive picture of this phenomenon and potential solutions to address it.

The fifth chapter, *Information Consumption and Trust*, examines the conditions influencing access to information, shaped by the media environment, the credibility of the news, and public preferences. This section begins with an overview of the evolution of research on uses and gratifications in the field of mass communication (Katz et al. 1973; Ruggiero 2000) before detailing how information consumption patterns have transformed since the beginning of the millennium. This transformation has resulted from technological and social changes, which have also led to an overabundance of information and triggered a crisis of confidence in traditional media.

1.1 Changes in the Post-media Sphere

The chapter offers an in-depth analysis of how Spaniards perceive their level of information and what their main preferences are, both in terms of coverage and topics. It provides details on differences across gender, political self-positioning, level of education, and geographic origin. It also highlights the nuances between the media normally used for information, those preferred for obtaining in-depth knowledge of a news topic, and those sought for higher-quality or more verified information. This section reveals key details about the audience characteristics of Spain's main media outlets, including television, radio, and both print and digital press.

In line with the tradition of research on media politicisation and selective exposure, the chapter also provides findings on public perceptions of this phenomenon. In today's socio-political context, the data collected underscores the bias of politicisation on the perception of media outlets that deviate from ideological lines, with a tendency to view them as leaning towards political extremes.

The sixth chapter, *Quality of Information and Democracy*, highlights the necessity of quality journalism as a fundamental pillar of democracy, beginning with a theoretical overview of the concept of journalistic quality and its evaluation. This section analyses the results of various studies that point to a decline in journalistic quality within the Spanish context, attributed to a lack of economic and political independence in the media, digital transformations, and low business investment in an environment marked by the effects of the crisis and precarious labour conditions.

In addition to expert and media professional analyses, the chapter includes an extensive public assessment of journalistic work. A concerning diagnosis is made regarding the deterioration of content quality in recent years. Survey data are used to detail both the main causes that, according to the public, contribute to the decline in quality and the content deemed most problematic, as well as the management practices that either hinder or promote journalistic quality.

Quality of Information and Democracy also includes proposals from various theorists on how to improve quality and outlines alternative solutions for citizens to find more relevant content. The survey further assesses public perception to determine who holds responsibility for information quality.

The seventh chapter, *Disruption in the Information Industry: Precariousness and Professional "Decapitalisation"*, focuses on the information industry and the dramatic changes it has experienced as a result of digitalisation and the continuous crises that have directly impacted not only the ways the profession is practised but also the conditions in which journalists work. This section analyses the effects of these global processes within the Spanish context, with the aim of contextualising the structural conditions upon which the information industry is based, including advertising investment, employment, business models, and corporate mergers.

This section delves into how the economic situation has directly influenced the structure of the journalistic profession and resulted in the "decapitalisation" of journalism's watchdog role (Palau-Sampio and López-García 2022, p. 5), with a marked increase in jobs directed towards corporate communication compared to the dwindling state of conventional media newsrooms. The chapter also underscores how the current working conditions for journalists clash with the professional values that have traditionally characterised the field, particularly journalistic autonomy, which is increasingly constrained by commercial and political pressures, as supported by various studies.

To further explore the state of the profession and the conditions under which journalism is practised, the final chapter includes testimony from 16 junior and senior Spanish professionals, participants in two focus groups held in 2024. This section brings together first-hand experiences and reflections, offering a detailed overview of the current professional context and the circumstances under which journalists work.

The concluding chapter summarises the most significant findings and proposes key lines of action to continue the research. There is an expressed need for further qualitative exploration of audience behaviour to better understand the changes occurring in the post-media sphere, reflected in patterns of media consumption.

The transformations within the ecosystem, driven by digitalisation, have impacted all levels and actors in an ongoing process of change. Thus, the study of these phenomena remains essential in the coming years, with a view to observing and understanding the complexity of the communication environment and its key actors, within the specific socio-political contexts in which they operate.

Open Access This chapter is licensed under the terms of the Creative Commons Attribution 4.0 International License (http://creativecommons.org/licenses/by/4.0/), which permits use, sharing, adaptation, distribution and reproduction in any medium or format, as long as you give appropriate credit to the original author(s) and the source, provide a link to the Creative Commons license and indicate if changes were made.

The images or other third party material in this chapter are included in the chapter's Creative Commons license, unless indicated otherwise in a credit line to the material. If material is not included in the chapter's Creative Commons license and your intended use is not permitted by statutory regulation or exceeds the permitted use, you will need to obtain permission directly from the copyright holder.

Chapter 2
The New Communication Ecosystem

2.1 How Communication Has Changed: The Impact of Digitalisation

The transformations that media and the communication process itself have undergone in recent decades are vast, varied, and of significant magnitude, making it challenging to encapsulate them all. However, if we had to highlight a specific element, the impact that digital technologies have had on the communication sector should probably be our focus. Digitalisation has fundamentally altered communication in many profound ways.

Sixty years have passed since the publication of *Understanding Media* by the Canadian philosopher Marshall McLuhan (1964). In this work, McLuhan offered an extensive view of media, describing them as "extensions of the human being", integral to all aspects of life. McLuhan's definition of media included not only the press, radio, and television (the primary social media of that era) but also communication devices such as the telephone and modes of transportation such as cars. Essentially, McLuhan depicted a society increasingly characterised by the pervasive presence of media in daily life.

At the time, McLuhan's broad description of media faced criticism for its expansive view and metaphorical-discursive approach, which lacked empirical support. However, the evolution of the communication ecosystem has demonstrated that McLuhan's insights are becoming a reality due to the systematisation of various forms of media and communication systems in society. These media—broadly defined—accompany us in activities that previously did not involve their presence or were conducted differently.

The proliferation of media closely relates to the hypothesis of mediatisation and its various manifestations. Schulz (2004) identifies four types of changes: extension, substitution, amalgamation, and adaptation.

1. Extension: Media are increasingly present in people's lives and more diverse in nature, effectively functioning as extensions of the human being, as McLuhan indicated.
2. Substitution: Media penetrate activities that were previously conducted without them, with new digital media replacing older forms (such as email replacing postal mail).
3. Amalgamation: Media are combined and mixed with other non-media activities, such as driving while listening to the radio or walking while looking at a mobile phone.
4. Adaptation: The specific weight of the media sector induces social changes of all kinds, requiring institutions and social actors to adapt to the logic of the media. This includes political leaders adapting their speeches, strategies, and even appearances to suit the preferences of television.

These changes are linked to the digitalisation process, which involves coding all types of information (textual, visual, auditory, various processes and applications, etc.) into binary code. Digitalisation facilitates the dissemination of all types of messages across various formats more rapidly and effectively than in the past. It enables the creation and distribution of content through any medium capable of reading and storing digital information, representing a significant shift from the previous analogue communication model (Calvo et al. 2024).

Traditional media were inextricably linked to specific formats: print to paper, radio to transistors, and television to screens. The recording and reproduction of content followed specific criteria and formats. In contrast, digital content always uses the same format—digital—and is encoded in binary. This means that text, images, moving images, vector processes, and various applications all ultimately follow the same coding system. And this, in turn, means that all of them can be distributed and displayed through any digital medium.

Now, we can read newspapers not just on computer screens but also on television or phone screens. Similarly, we can watch films on our smartphones or listen to music on our computers. Digital communication operates as an integrated whole, where any medium shares the same code and can potentially display and disseminate any type of digital content. In short, the entire communication system is doubly connected—through the Internet and digital code.

Just 25 years ago, the range of media options available to users was much smaller and more segmented according to the medium. Conventional media, such as press, radio, and television, derived their names from the medium that provided access to information, each with its specific logic and characteristics (López García 2015). Digital communication has managed to integrate and reproduce these logics, combining and disseminating them with much greater efficiency and flexibility, leading to a broader, more diverse, and more accessible offering in terms of technology (though access conditions are determined by content companies).

Public consumption habits have changed accordingly: both the number and audience of print newspapers have decreased, while television channels have increased, even as their global audience has declined. The same trend is observed in radio. All of this has had clear consequences for advertising revenue.

The change is even more evident in the leisure sector. Cinema has declined and relocated to audiovisual content platforms such as Netflix or Disney+, which have also absorbed part of the television audience. Video games have continued to grow and diversify, with an emphasis on online play, allowing users to compete against one another. The Internet has shifted from an expository period, where users consumed information presented by certain actors (particularly media and various organisations), to a focus on interpersonal communication and direct links with relevant social actors through social networks (Pérez et al. 2023).

2.2 Old and New Media: The Hybrid Communication Model

Both media and the communication ecosystem as a whole have undergone rapid change in recent years. In the past, the public had access to a relatively small number of large media outlets with large audiences and structures. These media established a relationship with the audience defined by the characteristics of communication emanating from them. The model was primarily unidirectional: media outlets sent the same message simultaneously to thousands or millions of people (media of *masses*, indeed). The audience's role was almost always passive: to receive and assimilate content. Rejection or interaction was linked to the public's sole decision: whether to consume a particular medium. Mechanisms of audience interaction, such as letters to the editor or listener calls, occupied a marginal space in the logic of media communication and were always filtered or controlled by the medium itself.

This situation has changed with the digital communication audience, which has much greater selection capacity: more media, accessible through more channels, with more segmented content that can be accessed at any time. The public replaces the *programming* logic with the *editing* logic: no longer subject to a rigid information menu dictated by the media (López García 2015). We can access information whenever and sometimes wherever we want, such as watching television news hours or days after it has been broadcast, consulting newspaper archives, or binge-watching entire seasons of TV series. This change has even modified the notion of boredom: now, the public is not bored due to a lack of options but because they are overwhelmed by choices and unsure what to select. The type of content consumption has also changed, tending to be more ephemeral and superficial than in the past (Carr 2011).

Consequently, the digital public is no longer just a passive "audience" consuming predetermined content. First, because their selection capacity, as seen, is much greater. Second, because they can interact with the medium and even create their own content. These factors (selection capacity and interaction possibilities) have led Manuel Castells (2009) to speak of "mass self-communication", or mass communication self-managed by users, a new communication model arising from the implementation of digital technologies.

This model, in summary, shows that McLuhan was correct and offers surprising derivatives of the notion of media as "extensions of the human being". These more abundant and diverse media contribute to the decline of the pre-existing communication ecosystem, characterised by the centrality of large media outlets. These outlets are now much smaller and compete with various communication entities, some media-related, many not, but all capable of capturing the public's attention and integrating it into logics beyond the flow of traditional mass media.

The communicative ecosystem is thus changing and complex, with enormous diversity. The pre-eminence of traditional media is eroded by the growing centrality of social networks as information sources, diluting journalism's social role as an agent that contextualises and selects messages from interested parties. The mediation capacity of journalists and benchmark media is diminished, if not eliminated, for some population groups. Generational, ideological, or socio-economic dissonances determine the distancing of large population groups from media discourses.

However, it is impossible to understand the current communication ecosystem without considering the continued role of media in setting the public agenda, either independently or as a reflection that grants credibility or at least visibility to other social actors. Media outlets are responsible for setting public debate; however, they can no longer do so independently of the opinions and interests of these actors, reflected through content circulating in the communication ecosystem. According to Chadwick (2013), we have thus arrived at a hybrid media system, characterised by the coexistence—sometimes contentious but practically complementary—of the traditional media system, which is more interested than ever in activities and messages from other environments, and the active, visible, and often segmented participation of new social actors emerging through social networks and other communication devices not controlled or predetermined by communication companies.

2.3 New Actors and Audiences

It is evident that social networks, when considered collectively, significantly alter the communicative capabilities of the Internet. Social networks enhance public interaction at various levels and simplify the content creation process. They also diversify the information available to the public, as well as its nature and origin. All these changes have profound implications for both the public and the media.

For the public, social networks increase the horizontality of communication, which contributes to democratising the process, at least in appearance. Any individual can create a profile on social networks and produce content that can potentially reach millions of people. Additionally, they can interact with other participants on social networks, whether they are individuals, institutions, or companies, with the not-often-justified hope of receiving a response.

2.3 New Actors and Audiences

However, behind the apparent democratisation of communication that these new interaction possibilities bring, new hierarchies emerge, or existing ones are adapted and perpetuated. The flow of communication generated on social networks often focuses around the most influential actors, those with the greatest capacity to reach the public. In this scenario, the media undoubtedly continue to occupy a key position. Additionally, individuals who already had significant visibility or social presence often see this reinforced on social networks.

Despite seeming to be a favourable scenario for the media, it is not entirely so. Here, the media lose their monopoly on mediation, which involves the selection, transmission, and interpretation of what is relevant. While the media still hold a central position in the communication ecosystem and remain the primary arbiters of what is important, they are no longer alone. They are joined by new social leaders, or influencers, who, though they may interact with the media in various ways, are not part of the traditional media and can maintain their own content agendas. What's more, they can attempt to have their agenda adopted by the media.

These new leaders increasingly build their popularity among the public independently of the media. Their visibility on social networks, rather than in traditional media, is what enables them to attract their own audience. This visibility always stems from a consistent characteristic: the user creates a profile, and from this profile and their activities on one or more social networks, they build a community around them. The media often engage with these figures only after they have achieved initial prominence; indeed, their visibility in networks draws media attention. These new social leaders, emerging from social networks and, at best, endorsed by the media, do not benefit from the inevitable journalistic mediation the media had in the previous scenario. The public now accesses information mainly through three channels:

- Search engines or AI tools that help them find answers to specific questions
- Recommendations of interesting content found on social networks
- Direct access to specific media outlets

The media do not control public activity on search engines or social media, yet this activity profoundly affects the public's perception of reality—a perception in which the media no longer hold as much sway as they once did. Both social networks and search engines contribute to greater content segmentation, driven by the public's interests, searches, or followed accounts, and by the content shown by social networks, which is in turn based on an algorithm trained according to their preference history—an increasingly refined filter bubble (Pariser 2011).

To remain relevant, or at least not disappear, in this context, the media must adapt to this logic, which necessarily involves relinquishing their previous role as the sole mediators for the public. The public of mass communication, which consumed the same content provided by large media outlets (Wolton 1992), is disappearing along with the media themselves, replaced by the homogeneously fragmented public of the Internet.

The structure of social networks leads the media to adapt their content to this new environment. This means, on one hand, accelerating news cycles according to public preferences, who become interested and disinterested in topics very quickly. This acceleration often results in simplified and poorly developed news and content. On the other hand, the media must offer content that interests the public. Unlike the era of the mass press, where the public response was less quantifiable, we now know exactly how the public reacts to any content and can quantify it with great precision. This reality forces many media outlets to cover topics and adopt perspectives based not on their journalistic relevance but on what works in terms of audience numbers. A factor that has always been present in media activities, but now more than ever, with significant implications for the structure of the media, its preferences, and its social role.

Finally, the significant audience fragmentation occurring should be noted. This is not only due to the aforementioned filter bubble, which arises from both the substantial selection capacity available and the algorithmic self-organisation of content based on user preferences. It is also a consequence of the audience's subdivision into increasingly smaller groups, linked by more specific criteria, distancing themselves entirely from the mass communication audience and its shared experiences from media consumption (Wolton 2000). These audiences are subdivided and segmented by multiple factors, which include:

- The vehicular language. While the Internet is global, global phenomena are largely confined to the main languages of exchange, particularly English, coexisting with audiences organised around the language they share.
- Specific interests. Contrary to the common information menu and large audiences typical of conventional media, the communication ecosystem is actually shaped by an enormous range of increasingly specific content, tailored to more specific audiences based on their thematic preferences.
- The generational factor. This is likely the most evident aspect of audience segmentation, highlighted by the contrast between younger and older generations. Both consumption habits and preferences show clearly differentiated patterns according to this criterion (Pérez et al. 2023).

2.4 The Ambivalence of Mediatisation

The scenario we have described leads to a contradictory conclusion. On one hand, technologically mediated communication has never been more present in people's lives. We are surrounded by communication devices that organise and structure our lives and relationships. We consume informative and entertainment content, establish social bonds and relationships, purchase all types of products, and even define and diversify our identity through digitally encoded technological devices, usually connected to the Internet. The media effectively function as extensions of individuals, who live in a permanently connected world, to such an extent that digital disconnection (Kaun and Treré 2020) begins to seem both a luxury and a chimera.

2.4 The Ambivalence of Mediatisation

All of this evidences a highly mediatised scenario. The concept of mediatisation, which emerged relatively recently (Mazzoleni and Schulz 1999), encompasses various intertwined phenomena, all connected by a common thread: the omnipresence of the media in contemporary societies. The most basic definition of mediatisation refers precisely to the fact that the media are becoming increasingly numerous and pervasive, extending across more layers and aspects of society.

Indeed, society is now organised and explained much more through media and technologically mediated communication systems than in the past; it is a society with a high degree of mediatisation. On the other hand, as we have also seen, the relative weight of the media in the classical sense (both conventional and their digital equivalents) is only decreasing, especially among certain highly connected groups who no longer directly engage with media content. Thus, we find ourselves in a state of mediatisation where the role of the media is diminishing and losing its central position (Bennett and Iyengar 2008).

However, this does not mean that the media lack significance in defining reality or even as a performative element of it. The media, when considered individually, have seen a decline in social importance as large audiences have dwindled; however, their social influence persists, often manifesting indirectly. Messages shared on social networks, frequently echoed by influencers, commonly originate from traditional media or, alternatively, they gain traction and are further disseminated by these media outlets.

In conclusion, when viewed collectively, the media still play a crucial role in shaping public opinion. Despite facing unprecedented competition and challenges in reaching a fragmented audience that is disengaged from public affairs (Zaller 1992) and whose capacity to focus on informational content has markedly decreased (Boczkowski and Mitchelstein 2015), there remains little doubt that the media continue to be the principal intermediaries between the public and power in its various forms. This is either because they determine what messages are conveyed to the public and how they are delivered or because they have a significant capacity to channel and amplify messages from the specific communication spaces of various social actors.

In this context, conventional media coexist with new digital communication platforms, many of which are extensions or offshoots of traditional media, as well as new forms of digital communication associated with individuals and organisations that now also distribute messages capable of reaching large audiences. This convergence forms a complex hybrid communication environment between conventional and new digital media (Chadwick 2013), where messages move in multiple directions and reach citizens through various channels. This chaotic landscape underlines a clear conclusion: social action is inevitably influenced by the logic of communication, irrespective of whether it is the media, social actors, or anonymous citizens driving the discourse.

Open Access This chapter is licensed under the terms of the Creative Commons Attribution 4.0 International License (http://creativecommons.org/licenses/by/4.0/), which permits use, sharing, adaptation, distribution and reproduction in any medium or format, as long as you give appropriate credit to the original author(s) and the source, provide a link to the Creative Commons license and indicate if changes were made.

The images or other third party material in this chapter are included in the chapter's Creative Commons license, unless indicated otherwise in a credit line to the material. If material is not included in the chapter's Creative Commons license and your intended use is not permitted by statutory regulation or exceeds the permitted use, you will need to obtain permission directly from the copyright holder.

Chapter 3
Fragmentation and Dissolution of the Public Sphere

3.1 The Public Space and Public Sphere

We have briefly reviewed how changes in communication significantly impact the structure and functioning of the communication ecosystem and the role of the media. However, these changes also affect the overall process of shaping public opinion, which will be discussed in this chapter.

Public opinion is the result of a highly complex process involving various social actors with diverse, often opposing perspectives (Crespi 2000). This process is inherently subject to continuous change. To better understand the parameters within which this social discourse occurs and its effects, we must examine two interrelated concepts that outline the scenario where this process of public opinion takes place: public space and public sphere.

When we refer to public space, we primarily mean a place, not a specific location, but a collection of spaces where public opinion is or can be generated. Public space is a space where public debate takes place, subject to public scrutiny, and where the actors participating in the public opinion process evolve. This "space" can be physical, such as city streets during a demonstration or a public assembly in a square, but it is fundamentally a conceptual term. A newspaper, television programme, or social media posts are also considered public space because the public (at least potentially) views what is narrated or occurs there.

In this public space, we find actors participating in public debate (politicians, journalists, opinion leaders) and spectators (the observing public) (Price 1994). The public sphere emerges from the interaction of social actors in the public space. Both concepts are defined in Jürgen Habermas' work *History and Criticism of Public Opinion* [1962] (1997), an analysis of the origins and evolution of public opinion that gave rise to bourgeois revolutions in the West. Habermas defines a public sphere with specific conditions and actors, typically operating in small spaces, in person, and with an active role.

These limited spaces (salons, cafes, and public assemblies) gradually gave way, following the bourgeois revolutions of the eighteenth and nineteenth centuries, to the public space that organises our modern democracies. This public space, organised by the mass media as interpreters of social reality and general mediators, led to a form of unidirectional communication, dictated by the economic and social elites, where public participation is almost always marginal or non-existent [1981] (1999). The mediated public sphere, developed in response to the needs of modern complex social systems characterised by intermediation (political and media)—inevitable if we want to fit in groups of millions of people organised in nation states of hundreds of thousands or millions of square kilometres—has been and continues to be strongly criticised in studies of public opinion and analyses of the media's role. We will revisit this issue.

As indicated, the public space is a place that can potentially host a public discussion contributing to the process of public opinion formation. However, for this space to become effective, it is not enough for it to exist; something must happen there. In summary, the social actors who lead the public opinion process must play a role there, just as the public must participate, even if only as passive spectators. The definition of the public sphere as a representation arises from the distinction between the place itself and the event that occurs there. Indeed, this notion of place and representation provides a valid metaphor to define both concepts: public space functions as a theatre where performances of all kinds may or may not take place, and the public sphere is the performance itself, with its actors and spectators.

Like the public space, the public sphere has its roots in pre-industrial societies before the bourgeois revolutions that opened the door to the contemporary world. In this earlier context, the public sphere, as interpreted by Habermas (1997), was a space progressively freed from the instances and prerogatives of power in the Old Regime. The public sphere, developed in informal social spaces (cafes, bars, civic meetings, festivities), allowed for open and free discussions between citizens, not subject to repressive power instances nor conditioned by inequalities or hierarchical relationships. Free and equal citizens would debate through rational discussion and seek decisions as a product of consensus. This discussion moved from private spaces to a public sphere that produced discourse and action (*lexis* and *praxis*, as Aristotle indicated and Hannah Arendt also recalls) and initially operated independently of power, later as an alternative and even substitute instance of constituted power.

In Arendt's view [1958] (1993), the public sphere derives from the model of social organisation. In the ancient world, the public sphere contrasts with the private sphere. In the private sphere, the individual seeks to satisfy basic needs and find private space within the family unit, differentiated from the public. The private, in this context, is defined as what individuals seek to hide from others' scrutiny. The public, on the other hand, is that which only makes sense if displayed in public, as in the case of a debate or discussion concerning the community. Only individuals who have their needs guaranteed and therefore their private space, could participate in the public sphere. According to Arendt, this grants them the necessary freedom to participate and the essential egalitarian condition for the public sphere to be composed of peers who, regardless of wealth or social position, can act freely in public space.

Both Arendt and Habermas, as can be seen, developed a definition of the public sphere in the past characterised by very similar features: the participants' freedom, their egalitarian condition, their disinterest in defending positions out of particular interest, and the search for a consensus beneficial to everyone. These characteristics, in the opinion of both, were clearly deteriorated by the evolution of the public sphere in contemporary societies, characterised by inevitable media mediation (López-García and Valera-Ordaz 2024).

3.2 The Mediasphere: The Public Media Sphere

The model of the public sphere—and public opinion—described by Habermas and Arendt ceased to be viable as the societies to which it applied evolved and became increasingly complex. This complexity was evident in their spatiotemporal dimensions: large nation-states with hundreds of thousands of square kilometres and millions of inhabitants. Additionally, the dimension of society that the participants in the public sphere sought to represent was a quantitatively minuscule minority in comparison.

Indeed, the public sphere of bourgeois societies of the Old Regime was limited to very small and specific spaces and populations. However, the societies resulting from the bourgeois revolutions necessarily required intermediary bodies capable of communicating between actors and spectators, even though political rights were initially limited to a very small sector of the population (adult men with a certain level of property). These intermediary instances were the social media, capable of becoming spokespersons for both power and society, privileged intermediaries between them, reaching the majority of the population in a relatively short period and condensing public discourse into something manageable and interpretable for citizens. Moreover, the extension of democratic rights became a constant in almost all Western nation-states throughout the nineteenth and twentieth centuries, requiring the media to adapt, gain complexity, and develop technological and communicative capacity.

Habermas and Arendt both agree on the diagnosis of the functioning and characteristics of the public sphere woven together by bourgeois societies, as well as on the reasons for its decline, which they attribute to the media (López-García and Valera-Ordaz 2024). According to Habermas, the media simplify and institutionalise messages, often resulting in the replacement of communication established in the previous public sphere, characterised by the interaction of free and rational individuals and the search for a consensus. The media cause the "psychosociological dissolution" of public opinion studies, which end up being confused with the media's published opinion. Public opinion is reduced to figures presented to citizens to explain what they supposedly think (polls, studies, laboratory experiments) emanating from the media's discourse (Sampedro 2023). The media establish themselves as pretended interpreters of social reality, functioning in practice as spokespersons for power, leaving little room for dialogue between people in a plural public sphere, which Habermas (1999) proposes to locate in what he calls "the world of life", precisely away from institutions, power, and the media.

Arendt [1958] (1993) also concludes that the public sphere loses its meaning in the era of mass society because it no longer serves as a space where all its actors can operate and express themselves in terms of equality but rather becomes a space predetermined and organised by the media. The media's importance, crucial early on in the analyses of democratic (and non-democratic) societies, enlightened in mass society. In such societies, the media become systematic and privileged intermediaries. Almost everything passes through them. If something does not pass through the media, it simply does not exist or holds marginal, limited importance in the eyes of citizens.

And how could it be otherwise? How could citizens realise that something is happening if the media do not tell them or tell it differently? This idea that the media are powerful not for telling us what to think about certain topics but for determining what topics to think about constitutes one of the most influential research lines on the media's social role in the twentieth century, the agenda-setting theory and its derivations (McCombs and Shaw 1972). Not surprisingly, this social role has been inextricably linked for decades to discussions about the media's effects on the public. The potentially enormous influence they have on citizens and their prescriptive capacity is so evident that most approaches focused on the media address and worry about their effects.

Similarly, analysing the functioning of public opinion is also determined by the central role of the media, widespread and indispensable mediators instrumentalised by the elites and directed at a citizenry that often is not so much manipulated against its will but simply does not pay much attention to what it is being told (Lippmann 1922; Zaller 1992).

The mediasphere, the public sphere agreed upon by and within the mass media, responds to very specific circumstances: the media, with immense audiences and great capacity to condense and interpret reality to the public, while having few mechanisms to interact with it, become both the stage for public opinion (the public space) and its privileged interpreters (the public sphere). The public discourse crafted by social actors is entirely a product of the media's discursive logic. In essence, it represents a highly mediated reality (Palau-Sampio and López-García 2022). According to Schlesinger (2020), the public sphere mediated by mass media, particularly the press and television, is characterised by the control of public discourse by communicators who are central to this media system, functioning as indispensable mediators.

Hence, we refer to this as the mediasphere, and Castells (2009) attributes to the media the crucial role of constituting "the space in which power is defined", which is what a public sphere colonised by the media and organised around their interests and discursive logic entails. The public sphere concentrated within the media does not propose a genuine debate or dialogue under minimally open and egalitarian conditions. Public opinion operates in an aggregated manner, as a result of messages emanating from power and assimilated by the public, with little possibility of proposing an alternative discursive public opinion (Sampedro 2000).

3.3 The Post-media Public Sphere

As highlighted in recent decades, digital technologies have extended and systematised their use in various applications and social environments. Communication has become inextricably linked to digitalisation. This implies that public opinion has transformed through a process occurring within a digital environment. Both the media and the mechanisms through which individuals access public debate are now digital, encompassing both the actors of the debate in the public sphere and its spectators. All are digitally connected, which means that the public debate as a whole has changed (Pérez et al. 2023).

This change manifests in two ways. Firstly, the public space, where the public opinion process occurs, has expanded, and its boundaries have blurred. This expansion allows anyone to take a more active role in these debates. Information is more accessible than ever, not just because there is more of it, but because it is easier to access through numerous mechanisms and devices. We have moved beyond the scenario where mass media held a monopoly on intermediation. Now, all participants and spectators of the public opinion process (Price 1994) can engage in public debate without necessarily passing through the media filter. While there is a risk that no one will hear an individual's voice, as the media still serve as powerful amplifiers, they no longer have the exclusive power to silence other voices.

Secondly, public space is fragmented from various perspectives (ideological, generational, socio-economic). These are smaller, more homogeneous spaces where the public debate of increasing numbers of citizens takes place. The multiplicity of media and communication sources allows the public to organise around the media and sources most aligned with their views (Sunstein 2019). This does not mean citizens only receive messages that reaffirm their existing beliefs. The process of polarisation, which will be discussed in the next chapter, is more complex. The public tends to pay more attention to messages that align with their views and to reject or ignore opposing messages, which often reach them filtered through negative lenses that minimise their impact (Bimber and Gil de Zúñiga 2022). The issue is not so much access to information but how each source or perspective on a specific issue is accessed. Thus, we find a public space that is both highly segmented—divided by affinity and access to information—and increasingly polarised around opposing views that are often presented as incompatible.

As a result, we reach a contradictory conclusion: the increase in informational pluralism and the multiplicity of messages resulting from digitalisation do not create a large, plural public space characterised by the exchange of opinions and the search for consensus (Schäfer 2015). On the contrary, the digital public sphere generates multiple public spaces and greater polarisation. And this conclusion undermines the early hopes that the Internet inspired, when "cyber-optimist" theories abounded (Lévy 2002; Jenkins 2008), asserting that the Internet would create a richer and more diverse public space, where debates with active citizen participation would take place, and decisions made would reflect the general interest. They initially believed that the Internet and new digital communication would address the shortcomings and problems of mass society, whose public debate was practically monopolised by intermediaries (Rheingold 2002; Jenkins 2008).

In contrast, cyber-pessimists (Lanier 2011; Morozov 2011) later emerged, arguing that the Internet also led to the simplification and polarisation of public debate. They noted that the undeniable virtues of digital technologies—their capacity to enhance communication in its various forms—were either not used by the majority of citizens or were instrumentalised for the benefit of a few individuals and institutions, effectively directing public debate or, even worse, generating so much noise these debates—understood to be a rational exchange of arguments whose objective was to reach consensus—became impracticable (Pérez et al. 2023). The crisis of intermediation has evolved into a crisis of public space, leading to the paradoxical situation of yearning for the previous scenario, with all its problems and insufficiencies, because media intermediation at least guaranteed a recognisable dialogue that established a clearly delimited playing field (a public space) (Bimber and Gil de Zúñiga 2022).

Traditional media have lost influence, audience, and credibility, as will be discussed in the following chapters. Parallel to this decline, the possibilities for message distribution via social networks have opened the door to new political and social actors, diversifying the public sphere. However, this has also lowered the standards that were previously imposed by the media, but not by these new actors, for message dissemination, in terms of their quality, informative value, and respect for truthfulness or different groups. Consequently, these new messages often do not promote consensus and unity but rather contribute to polarisation and fragmentation (Sunstein 2019).

The post-media public sphere does not align with Habermas' idea of an inclusive public sphere of debate and consensus (Habermas 1997). This is mainly due to two factors (Bennett and Pfetsch 2018): first, the multiplication of messages, media, and information sources has increased noise and voice dispersion in the public space. Second, the fragmentation of audiences reorganises around homogeneous, self-referential public spheres that barely interact with the "exterior", functioning as echo chambers into which alternative viewpoints rarely enter (Dahlgren 2005). Simultaneously, trust in institutions that held power and credibility in the "media-sphere", particularly the media themselves, is declining, and the same can be said of their influence (Palau-Sampio and López-García 2022). As a result, individuals, lacking the indisputable and recognisable references of the past, tend to structure themselves in increasingly singular and specific environments, comfortingly predictable, where reality is interpreted according to each one's biases (Llorca-Abad and Gamir-Ríos 2023). It is not surprising that this scenario invalidates any notion of rational interaction between equals seeking consensus, as Habermas (1998) proposed in outlining the space of deliberative democracy that characterises the public sphere (Sampedro 2023). Indeed, Habermas himself reaches this conclusion in a

3.3 The Post-media Public Sphere

recent work (2023), considering that the democratic and deliberative potential of new digital communication platforms is currently inactivated by the persistence of the economic interests of platform owners and the often superficial, partisan, and demagogic uses to which they are put.

In summary, 30 years have passed since the Internet began to spread rapidly among the population, and—generously—20 years since the digitalisation process became widespread among the media sector, and its effects on content consumption became evident. In this short period, we have gone from severely critiquing the "mediasphere" scenario controlled by mass media, which issued a unidirectional and univocal message to the entire population, to being scandalised by the current fragmentary and partisan chaos, to the extent that many question the very existence of the public sphere. Dahlgren (2005) suggests replacing it with the concept of civic culture. Bennett and Pfetsch (2018) believe that its framework should be reformulated, as it is no longer characterised by a coherent and self-sufficient public sphere and media system. Bimber and Gil de Zúñiga (2022) argue that the public in this public sphere is incapable of unravelling the forces shaping public debate, reminiscent of Lippmann's (1922) critique of public opinion in mass society controlled by the media. Schlesinger (2020) prefers to speak directly of a post-public sphere, a space primarily generating doubts and uncertainty, since the crisis of media intermediation is not replaced by a comparable intermediation model, nor can it be considered that current public debate is characterised by the search for a Habermasian, rational consensus.

Pessimism regarding the public sphere model (or "non-public sphere" if preferred) is such that some researchers nostalgically evaluate the previous mediasphere scenario, openly longing for it. Like Wolton, who once defended the role of mass media, particularly television, in social and cultural cohesion (Wolton 1992), bitterly lamenting its decline at the hands of the limitless choice diversity of the Internet (Wolton 2000), similar sentiments are now seen in many reflections arising from the debate on disinformation, polarisation, or the many shortcomings of the hybrid media system, longing for a past time when mass media were considered better.

However, whether or not "every past public sphere" (or at least that of the media) was better, the truth is that this is not the world we have now, nor is it the public sphere we currently possess. And above all, it is entirely unfeasible to return to the previous scenario. In the post-media public sphere, the media still play a role, but they are no longer as decisive as they once were and no longer monopolise the interpretation of reality for the public. Alongside the media, we find new actors or familiar ones from the past public sphere, who have now redefined their roles and relationships with the public. These actors not only interact among themselves or with the public but also with the media, which now serve as references and significant actors in social networks (Bruns 2023). We also find new approaches, relationships, interests, and ways of communicating and interacting. It is a highly complex scenario that is now unfolding, and we are only beginning to understand some parameters, as Habermas (2023) reminds us, despite his critique of the digital public sphere, considering that the problem may largely be a matter of the public's digital literacy, which has rapidly accessed new and changing technologies.

Open Access This chapter is licensed under the terms of the Creative Commons Attribution 4.0 International License (http://creativecommons.org/licenses/by/4.0/), which permits use, sharing, adaptation, distribution and reproduction in any medium or format, as long as you give appropriate credit to the original author(s) and the source, provide a link to the Creative Commons license and indicate if changes were made.

The images or other third party material in this chapter are included in the chapter's Creative Commons license, unless indicated otherwise in a credit line to the material. If material is not included in the chapter's Creative Commons license and your intended use is not permitted by statutory regulation or exceeds the permitted use, you will need to obtain permission directly from the copyright holder.

Chapter 4
Challenges in a Hostile Scenario

In the last decade, the debate on the resilience of Western democracies has been shaped by the threats of polarisation, disinformation, and the rise of populism (Svolik 2019; Tenove 2020; Schia and Gjesvik 2020; McKay and Tenove 2021; Schünemann 2022). This threat is particularly concerning when these forces combine within the hybrid media ecosystem (Chadwick 2013), where the dynamics of division, fragmentation, and distortion pose a significant risk to the effective functioning of representative democracy, which relies on citizens' votes (Callander and Carbajal 2022).

While none of these phenomena is entirely new (Rid 2020; DiMaggio et al. 1996), their emergence within a hybrid context—where traditional media logic intersects with that of digital communication (Chadwick 2013; Mazzoleni 2014)—introduces uncertain risks. Disinformation strategies, in particular, have never had such an extensive global reach as they do today, driven by a confluence of technological, political, and social factors that reinforce one another (Klimkiewicz 2019). However, some authors caution that it is misleading to attribute the causes of the threats to democracy solely to digital communication (Waisbord 2020). To properly analyse these challenges, it is essential to contextualise the three dynamics discussed in the following sections. Our objective is to examine their manifestations within the Spanish context, drawing on data from a survey of 1200 people.

© The Author(s) 2025
D. Palau-Sampio, G. López-García, *News, Media, and Communication in a Polarized World*, SpringerBriefs in Political Science,
https://doi.org/10.1007/978-3-031-86620-3_4

4.1 Ideological and Emotional Distancing, Belonging, and Exclusion

4.1.1 Polarisation

Political polarisation refers to the deepening ideological and programmatic divides between different political parties, making their positions increasingly irreconcilable (Sani and Sartori 1983). This growing divide leads to greater social fragmentation and poses a significant threat to democracy's resilience: "In healthy democracies, opposing sides are seen as political adversaries to compete against and at times to negotiate with. In deeply polarized democracies, the other side comes to be seen as an enemy needing to be vanquished" (McCoy 2019). While political polarisation is generally viewed as a problematic phenomenon from a normative perspective (Reiljan 2020), some degree of polarisation is deemed necessary to foster competition between parties and to provide voters with distinct alternatives (Barber and McCarty 2015; McCoy et al. 2018).

Approaches to polarisation reveal its dual nature, as it serves both as a description of a political state (McCoy et al. 2018) and as a process (DiMaggio et al. 1996; Callander and Carbajal 2022). In this sense, polarisation can be seen as a long-term development initiated by elites and eventually adopted by voters, who increasingly base their political views not on the principles of the parties they support, but on the rejection of their opponents' views (Callander and Carbajal 2022; Abramowitz and Webster 2016).

The concept of political polarisation is far from straightforward, as it encompasses various phenomena that involve ideological or emotional divides. Firstly, it can manifest as "a growing alignment of political parties around increasingly distant positions" (Miller 2020, p. 13). This form, known as ideological polarisation, relates to how parties and their supporters position themselves on a spectrum, typically involving left-right or nationalism-centralism identification. Symbolic polarisation, on the other hand, pertains to specific stances on issues like economic policy, immigration, or equality policies.

Second, affective polarisation transcends the positioning of parties and their voters on a certain scale to focus "on the feelings that parties and political leaders arouse" (Miller 2020: 13). It therefore implies an emotional attachment to supporters of one's own group and hostility towards those of opposing groups (Iyengar et al. 2012). This process goes beyond classic ideological polarisation, in the sense that an increase in inter-partisan hostilities may not be reflected in higher levels of ideological disagreements among citizens and may have more devastating consequences (Torcal and Comellas 2022).

Regarding the relationship between these two phenomena, there is no consensus. Some perspectives suggest a link, arguing that affective polarisation stems from partisan identities and the alignment of other social identities with them (Iyengar et al. 2012). Conversely, other viewpoints assert that ideological polarisation is one of the primary forces driving the polarisation of feelings towards political parties (Torcal and Comellas 2022). Moreover, affective polarisation can stem from non-partisan identities that divide the world into in-groups and out-groups, such as religion or ethnicity (Westwood et al. 2018).

Recent studies have demonstrated a growing political polarisation in the US, Europe, and Latin America (Hetherington 2009; McCoy et al. 2018; Svolik 2019). Casal and Rama note that Europe has experienced a steady rise in polarisation since the 1960s, which became particularly pronounced from the 1990s onwards, coinciding with the emergence of radical (populist) parties and a significant increase in votes for anti-establishment parties (2021).

Since the turn of the century, ideological polarisation in Spain has surged by nearly one and a half points on a scale of 0 to 10 (with 10 representing the greatest polarisation), based on data from the Centre for Sociological Research (CIS). The score increased from 3.75 in 2000 to 5.10 in 2019 (Simón 2020). The widest left-right divide during this period was observed between 2015 and 2016, "when the two-party system transitioned to a four-party system. Polarisation along the territorial axis was particularly pronounced between 2008 and 2011" (Simón 2020, pp. 453–454).

The identification of 2019 as peak polarisation is not accidental, considering three key factors (López García and Domínguez 2021). Firstly, the decline of the two-party system led to a drop in voting intention for the two main parties, from their peak in 2008 (when PSOE and PP jointly accounted for 83.8% of the vote) to their collapse in 2015, just 8 years later, when they fell to 50.7%. The emergence of two new parties, Podemos and Ciudadanos—which for the first time challenged the stability of the two-party system and sought to compete with PSOE and PP for electoral space—resulted in a greater dispersion of votes and a noticeable increase of polarisation in the rhetoric and opinions of politicians, the media, and citizens.

Secondly, the Catalan independence crisis, which peaked between 2017 and 2019, intensified polarisation, particularly in Catalonia but also beyond. This escalation was evident in the breakdown of social cohesion and the unprecedented judicialisation of politics in a democratic context, culminating in several pro-independence leaders fleeing Spain, including the then-President of the Generalitat of Catalonia, Carles Puigdemont.

Finally, the rise of VOX, a far-right party entering Congress for the first time since 1979, and its subsequent consolidation as the third political force in the second election of 2019 further fragmented an electorate that, just a decade earlier, had been part of a seemingly stable two-party system. Indeed, the first election in 2019, which followed the Socialist Party's ascent to power after Pedro Sánchez ousted Mariano Rajoy in the first successful vote of no confidence in Spain's democratic history, marked the peak of the two-party system's decline (45.4% between PSOE and PP). However, there has been a notable recovery, especially in the 2023 election (64.8% between PP and PSOE), with figures reminiscent of earlier elections, such as those in 1977 and 1989. The following graph shows the evolution of the Spanish electorate (Fig. 4.1).

The dynamics of fragmentation that have dominated public life in recent years prompted the Fundación del Español Urgente, in collaboration with the Real Academia de la Lengua and the EFE Agency, to select "polarisation" as the word of the year for 2023. This choice reflects the frequent reference to "situations where

Fig. 4.1 Bipartisanship in Spain: Percentage of votes for the two main political parties, 1977–2023. Source: prepared by the authors

there are two very distinct or distant options or activities, often with implicit notions of tension and confrontation" (FundéuRAE 2023).

Ideological polarisation is evident not only in the left-right divide but also in the alignment on various public agenda issues. In this regard, one of the most significant aspects is the stance on the territorial issue—whether people identify with their autonomous community or with Spain as a whole—where polarisation increased from 3.75 in 2008 to 5.04 in 2016 (Miller 2020). This level of polarisation surpasses that observed around other specific policies. Thus, territorial polarisation is two to three times greater than polarisation on issues such as taxes and immigration, with the latter being "about six times greater than polarisation around public health and about fifteen times greater than the negligible polarisation around services" (Miller 2020, p. 15).

Several studies indicate a high level of affective polarisation in southern Europe, particularly in Spain, Portugal, and Greece (Gidron et al. 2020). This suggests that the region merits increased focus on this issue, especially given its intersection with the rise of new radical parties amid growing partisan fragmentation and electoral volatility (Torcal and Comellas 2022). Similarly, a study by the Mercator Forum Migration and Democracy (MIDEM) and the Technische Universität Dresden ranked Italy highest in affective polarisation (Herold et al. 2024), with Spain occupying intermediate positions alongside Germany and Hungary.

Miller and Torcal (2020) present an analysis of affective polarisation in Spain between 1993 and 2019, focusing on sentiments towards political leaders. Their study identifies three election years with notable increases in polarisation: 1996, 2008, and 2015. In 2008, in particular, negative sentiments towards the opposing leaders were especially pronounced, although positive feelings towards one's own leader were more dominant.

Factors such as political or economic crises and the feeling of grievance and injustice that cause resentment are presented as triggers of polarisation (McCoy et al. 2018). In Spain, the last two periods of increased polarisation are clearly connected: the 2008 crisis led to higher unemployment and widened economic disparities, while in 2015, the fragmentation of the party system became apparent, alongside the rise of Podemos and Ciudadanos in the political landscape.

As several authors have pointed out, severe polarisation poses serious risks by threatening essential aspects of democratic processes, such as commitment, consensus, and tolerance. It also undermines citizens' trust in institutions (McCoy et al. 2018). This makes it harder to reach the agreements and compromises necessary to pass laws and budgets, promote public policies, or renew institutions, as illustrated by the stalled renewal of the General Council of the Judiciary in Spain (Marcos 2024).

The drivers of polarisation are closely linked to the dynamics of populism. One hallmark of severe polarisation is the Manichaean and moralising nature of political discourse (McCoy and Somer 2019), which fosters a social divide of "us" versus "them" (McCoy et al. 2018), and the identification of a virtuous populace against a corrupt elite (Mudde and Kaltwasser 2017). In this context, the rise of populism is seen as promoting a polarising, Manichaean rhetoric between immoral elites and the virtuous people (Mudde 2007).

4.1.2 Populism

When approaching the concept of populism, the first thing to determine is the perspective from which it is being analysed, as several conceptualisations exist. Bobba (2023) identifies three main approaches:

– Populism as an *ideology*, which divides society and its leaders between good and bad according to a set of precepts. In this sense, populism is seen as a "thin ideology" opposed to "full ideologies" (Freeden 1996, cited in Bobba 2023), meaning it does not develop a comprehensive worldview but is integrated and complemented by one of the "full ideologies" (e.g. Marxism, neoliberalism, fascism).
– Populism as a *political strategy*, a specific way of competing for political power and public favour, as well as a method of political action once power has been achieved.
– Finally, we can also classify populism as a *communicative style*, a way of addressing and interacting with the population. In this context, the form and communication tools used to reach the audience are as important, if not more so, than the content itself, as populist practices often involve simplifying messages and replacing rational discourse with emotional appeals (Crespi 2000).

Populist movements, as outlined by Taguieff (2002, pp. 125–135), can be analysed based on two fundamental categories:

– Populism as a protest movement characterised by the rejection of traditional politics and representative democracy. Two key features define this type: first, anti-intellectualism, where elites are dismissed as having held power behind the scenes, while "popular wisdom" is elevated to an almost mythical status. And second, the hyper-personalisation of the leader, who is viewed as uniquely capable of bridging the gap between the people and their representatives. Unlike tra-

ditional elites, this leader is believed to genuinely understand and embody the will of the people.
- Identity populism, or national populism, is strongly associated with the leader's appeal to "the people" and the notion of the nation being under threat from various dangers that could undermine its true nature. This concept is captured in the slogan "The French First" used by the French National Front and later adopted by many European far-right movements, including in Spain. Using the French National Front as an example, Taguieff identifies key aspects of this approach:
  - (a) The leader's political appeal is seen as a direct and personal call to "the people", positioning the leader as a unique interpreter of the popular will, embodying the idea of "everything with the people but without the people" in relation to the movement's ideological and social foundations.
  - (b) As a result, the appeal to "the people" is presented as inclusive, transcending social classes, ideological divisions, or cultural categories. This aligns with rhetoric that praises the "good people" of each nation—whether Spanish, French, German, or others, in their specific contexts— to position the populist movement as a unifying force motivated by higher ideals and national interests.
  - (c) The movement appeals to an "authentic" population, perceived as "simple", "honest", and "healthy", in contrast to the perceived corruption and detachment of traditional political parties. This is a clearly "anti-establishment" stance that attempts to present the populist movement (after all, this is the basis of all populism) as emerging "from the bottom", rooted in genuine national interests and popular wisdom, in direct opposition to elites and established political structures.
  - (d) The appeal to a purifying or saving rupture, understood as a dual movement of disruption and change. This involves a break with the existing political system as a necessary step to achieve "genuine change", in contrast to the superficial "changes of nuance" or the cosmetic "change everything so that everything stays the same" approach typically associated with political action.
  - (e) Lastly, the appeal for the unification of the people under the supreme principle of national unity, which serves both as a positive ideal and as a basis for exclusion. This form of nationalism asserts the homogeneity of the nation and its people, defining them in opposition to those considered outsiders, who may include immigrants (or specific groups of immigrants), Jews, homosexuals, and others.

Populism has significantly strengthened in recent years across its three dimensions—ideological, as a political strategy, and as a communication model—due to several key factors:
- The spread of digital technologies and their use in increasingly varied communication formats, which are easily accessible to both creators and the public. This

4.1 Ideological and Emotional Distancing, Belonging, and Exclusion

trend is especially noticeable on social media, where populist leaders have found a fertile ground and a privileged platform.
- The crisis of political representation, prompting a search for new solutions and the emergence of new leadership, as well as the adaptation of existing leaders to the populist style.
- The degradation of democratic and institutional politics, which has facilitated the rise of political proposals that distort democratic procedures, perceiving them as ineffective for political action or citizen engagement. Populism criticises representative democracy for being insufficiently democratic and for getting lost in ineffective processes.

4.1.3 Testing Populism and Polarisation

A survey conducted with 1200 participants in Spain, as part of the project "Informational Confusion: Precarious Quality, Over(dis)information, and Polarisation" (CIAICO2021/125), aimed to measure the prevalence of two significant phenomena in Spanish politics over the last decade: polarisation and populism. Twelve statements were presented to the participants, each associated with these phenomena, to determine the level of agreement or disagreement, as illustrated in Table 4.1.

Table 4.1 Degree of agreement or disagreement with the following statements (%)

Statement		Agree	Disagree
Populism	The political class acts in its own interests rather than for the public good	87.7	12.3
	Governments disregard the interests of the people when making decisions	78.4	21.6
	The financial sector controls the democratic system	80.2	19.8
	Traditional media (press, radio, television) manipulate information	77.0	23.0
	International organisations (e.g. European Union, International Monetary Fund) exert excessive control over the country	53.3	46.7
Polarisation	Society has lost traditional Spanish values, which should be restored	56.4	43.6
	Equality policies aim to balance the rights of men and women	63.5	36.5
	The effects of heat waves are overstated to support climate change theories	35.6	64.4
	The issue of squatting in Spain is minor and exaggerated by certain interests	34.4	65.6
	Immigrants have a privileged status compared to Spanish citizens	43.6	56.4
	Pandemic restrictions were a response to a unique health crisis rather than an attempt at control	72.2	27.8
	Recognition of sexual diversity (gay, lesbian, bisexual, and transgender) represents progress in human rights	81.4	18.6

The five statements in the survey related to populism address various representations of political, economic, or media elites, focusing on how these elites' power might negatively impact citizens' freedoms or well-being. One statement addressing the influence of international institutions on the country's sovereignty was also included. More than three-quarters of those surveyed agreed with the first four statements, and more than half of them agreed with the last.

The statement that achieved the highest level of agreement was "The political class acts in its own interests rather than for the public good" (87.7%). This indicates a significant disconnect between the public and political leaders, echoing survey findings that show widespread distrust (55.3%) and frustration (40.3%) with politics (CIS 2024). In contrast to the majority opinion, 12.3% of respondents disagreed.

This view of the political class was fairly homogeneous in terms of gender, age, population size, and educational level. However, political self-positioning showed that the far left was the furthest from the average (74.6%), while the statement had almost total unanimity on the right (95.6%), eight points ahead of the most extreme positions. When analysed by autonomous community, this sentiment is most prevalent in the Balearic Islands (96.9%), Extremadura (96.3%), and Cantabria (96.3%), despite their varying socio-economic contexts.

The statement "Governments disregard the interests of the people when making decisions" was supported by nearly eight out of ten citizens (78.4%). Interestingly, those on the right (89%) expressed stronger agreement, three points above the far right (86%). Education level also influenced agreement, with over 80% of those without a university degree supporting the statement. Younger respondents, particularly those under 25 (69.4%), showed the least agreement. This sentiment was particularly strong in less populated or peripheral regions such as Extremadura (92.6%), Castilla y León (86.2%), and Aragón (85.3%).

The Financial Sector's Influence Over Democratic Structures
The second statement that garnered the greatest agreement among the population asserts that the financial sector controls the democratic system, reflecting citizens' views on the impact of economic power on Spain's democratic institutions. This view was supported by eight out of ten citizens (80.2%), while 19.8% disagreed. Women were more likely to support this view (83.2%) compared to men (77%), by five percentage points. Support was also higher among the 35 to 64 age group, especially those aged 45 to 55 (86.5%).

This perception was notably stronger in some of Spain's wealthiest regions, such as the Basque Country (88.1%) and Catalonia (87.7%). In contrast, Madrid (71.3%) had one of the highest levels of disagreement. Political ideology also plays a significant role, with support for the statement ranging from 91.5% on the far left to 56.1% on the far right, showing a 35-point difference. This ideological divide is further evident between the right and centre-right, with a gap exceeding fifteen points. While the majority of non-believers (89.3%) and atheists (85.1%) supported the idea that economic power interferes with democratic institutions, practising Catholics were nine points below the average, with 71.4% in agreement.

Media and Manipulation

The fourth of the statements examined in the survey addresses the manipulative power of traditional media, specifically the press, radio, and television. A significant 77% of respondents agreed that these media outlets "manipulate information", while 23% disagreed. In contrast to perceptions of economic power, this view was more prevalent among men (79.8%) than women (74.4%). From a generational standpoint, those over 65 years of age (80.6%) were the most likely to agree, followed by individuals under 25 (78.4%). Ideological self-identification also played a role, with the far right showing the highest agreement (86%), exceeding the average by nine percentage points, followed by those identifying as right-wing (80%). Support for this statement was particularly strong in single-province communities, especially Cantabria (93.3%), followed by La Rioja (87.5%), Murcia, and Asturias (both 84.6%). Among those with master's or doctoral degrees (81.1%), as well as individuals who identified as indifferent (83.9%) or atheist (83.4%), agreement was notably higher.

Although not as strongly as the statements focused on the Spanish context, the issue of the influence that international organisations, such as the European Union or the International Monetary Fund, exert over the country still gained the agreement of over half of the respondents. Specifically, 53.3% believe that these institutions have "excessive control over the country", while 46.7% disagreed. Ideological alignment played a significant role here, with the far right showing 68.4% support for this view, 15 points above the average, and 20 points ahead of the left (48%), which expressed the most disagreement with the idea of such external interference.

Gender and generational differences were notable, with women (56.6%) and individuals aged between 55 and 64 (61.9%) more likely to perceive external power influences, compared to younger groups, such as those aged 25 to 34 (43.8%) or under 25 (46.3%). Atheists (56.4%) and those with master's or doctoral degrees (56.1%) showed the most disagreement with this statement, in contrast to non-practising Catholics (43.2%), followers of other religions (40.9%), and those with only primary education (29.9%). Regionally, the Basque Country (67.8%) and Cantabria (66.7%) were the most critical of external interference, with this sentiment also prevalent in towns with populations over 50,000.

4.1.3.1 Social Division on Key Issues

Seven of the statements in the survey aimed to assess the levels of social polarisation around key issues, reflecting indicators (Miller 2020) and topics currently on the public agenda, such as gender equality, sexual diversity policies, migration, housing, the environment, and pandemic measures. Additionally, an identity-related question was posed, as this has been one of the most polarising topics (Miller 2020).

With the exception of the statement about sexual identity progressing human rights, which is supported by over eight in ten Spaniards, and the measures taken during the pandemic, seen by more than seven out of ten as an adequate response to an exceptional health situation, the statements reflect a scenario of division: 40% of the population versus the remaining 60%.

The two most divisive statements refer to Spanish identity and migration. In the first instance, 56.4% of respondents agree with the notion that "society has lost traditional Spanish values, which should be restored", while 43.6% disagree. Although gender and population size are not significant factors in this case, ideological alignment plays a crucial role, with a stark contrast of more than 50 percentage points between the far left (31.5%) and the right (82.5%). A similar gap is observed between the left (39.3%) and right (79.1%), with the centre holding a more balanced position (64%). Among the autonomous communities, Extremadura (74.1%) and Aragón (70.6%) show the highest support for the need to restore traditional Spanish values, whereas communities such as La Rioja (12.5%), the Balearic Islands (40.6%), Catalonia (43.6%), and Navarre (44.4%) show less support. Interestingly, in contrast to these regions, the Basque Country, known for its strong nationalist sentiment, shows above-average support (61%) for the restoration of traditional Spanish values.

The generational factor also plays a significant role, with older individuals—particularly those over the age of 44—showing higher levels of agreement (64.6%), while younger generations tend to disagree more frequently. Among those aged 16 to 24, agreement falls below 40%, and in the next age group, it reaches only 44.4%. Educational attainment and religious beliefs are also influential. Those with less than primary education (85.7%) or only primary education (71%) show much higher levels of agreement than individuals with a master's degree or doctorate (41.2%). Additionally, those who identify as Catholic, whether practising (74.4%) or non-practising (69.1%), are twice as likely to agree with the statement compared to atheists (33.7%).

Migration

The statement "Immigrants have a privileged status compared to Spanish citizens" reveals a clear divide in Spanish society, with 43.6% of citizens agreeing and 56.4% disagreeing. Women are slightly more convinced of this perceived privilege (45.8%). Younger respondents, particularly those between 25 and 34 years old (68%), tend to disagree more strongly, contrasting with the support levels among the 45 to 54 age group (50.7%) and those aged 55 to 64 (49.2%). People living in towns with fewer than 10,000 inhabitants are more likely to believe in this privilege (49.4%), a full 10 points higher than those in towns with up to 50,000 inhabitants (39.4%).

Political ideology is crucial in shaping views on this issue, with extreme ends of the spectrum showing opposite perceptions. While 79.2% of those on the far left reject this statement, support rises to 78.9% among the far right. This aligns with the positions of VOX, a party that represents this electorate (Olmos-Alcaraz 2022), and advocates for the expulsion of irregular migrants and the elimination of subsidies to non-governmental organisations (NGOs), as proposed in the Congress of Deputies in April 2024 (Europa Press 2024). Among right-wing supporters, agreement towards the statement about supposed privileges of immigrants stands at 68.1%, which is 25 points above the national average. One of the consequences of parties

4.1 Ideological and Emotional Distancing, Belonging, and Exclusion

like VOX is the influence they exert on traditional conservative parties, as seen in the radicalisation of the PP's discourse during the closing of the Catalan electoral campaign in an attempt to compete with VOX for voters (García 2024). In fact, polarisation related to migration has been one of the fastest growing since 2008 (Miller 2020).

Similarly, among those who identify as left wing, rejection of the statement that immigrants have a privileged position prevails (76%). In contrast, agreement with the statement exceeds the average by 25 percentage points among right-wing individuals (68.1%), highlighting the critical stance on immigration prevalent among the most conservative voters. Educational background and religious affiliation are also significant factors in shaping opinions on this issue. Support for the idea that immigrants are privileged among those with a master's degree or doctorate (23.6%) is much lower than that of university graduates (35.7%). Among Catholics, both practising (58.6%) and non-practising (53.3%), the agreement is double that of atheists (28.7%) or agnostics (29%).

When analysing agreement with this statement across autonomous communities, the highest levels of support are found in Aragón (61.8%), Castilla y León (53.8%), and the Basque Country (50.8%). Paradoxically, none of these regions is among the three (Madrid, Catalonia, and the Valencian Community) that had the highest levels of migration in 2022 (EFE 2024). Conversely, in regions with the lowest levels of immigration, such as La Rioja (37.5%), Extremadura (33.3%), and Cantabria (40%), agreement with the statement is below average.

Gender Equality and Climate Change

The statement that "equality policies aim to balance the rights of men and women" garners agreement from nearly two-thirds of respondents (63.5%), while just over a third (36.5%) express disagreement. Those who disagree tend to be concentrated within specific demographic groups, notably people aged 35 to 44 (41.6%) and those with ideological affiliations to the far right (64.9%) and the right (60.4%). These figures suggest that equality policies have become a focal point of tension not only between the right and the left but also within the right itself. Thus, these policies are often seen as a symbol of progressive politics identified with feminism and are perceived as "a sort of hegemonic common enemy" endowed with "a destruction power that threatens the social order" (Cabezas Fernández et al. 2023, §45).

On the other hand, from the opposite perspective, the statement garners support from eight out of ten respondents who identify as left-wing or far-left, with rejection from the conservative sector being three times lower. While educational level is not a determining factor, religious affiliation is, with practising Catholics (56.4%) and those of other faiths (45.5%) showing lower than average agreement. In contrast, atheists (75.7%) and agnostics (69.4%) express much higher levels of agreement. By autonomous community, La Rioja (75%), the Basque Country (74.6%), and Catalonia (71.3%) are the most supportive of this statement, compared to respondents from Castilla La Mancha (52.3%), Aragón (52.9%), or Castilla y León (55.4%).

Climate change has become one of the most polarising issues in Europe (Herold et al. 2024). Reflecting this, respondents were asked to state their position on the statement: "The effects of heat waves are overstated to support climate change theories". Overall, 35.6% agreed with this statement, while 64.4% disagreed. However, deeper analysis reveals distinct profiles for each stance. Ideology strongly influences agreement, with 70.2% of those on the far right agreeing with the statement, compared to just 18.6% on the left and 24.6% on the far left. Unlike other issues such as national identity, migration, or equality policies, agreement on this statement shows a nearly 20-point gap between the right (51.6%) and the far right (70.2%).

Those most critical of the statement on climate change are aged 25 to 34 (26.1%), which is nine points below the average. Conversely, residents in towns with fewer than 10,000 inhabitants (39.7%) are more likely to agree. Educational level also influences opinions, with those holding a master's or doctoral degree (27.7%), as well as atheists (23.8%) and agnostics (24.2%), showing less support for the idea that the effects of heat waves are overstated to justify climate change.

Squatting and Housing

Housing has emerged as the second most pressing concern for Spaniards (21.2%), according to the June 2024 barometer from the Centre for Sociological Research, coming only behind general political issues and surpassing concerns like unemployment and economic conditions (CIS 2024). Various studies highlight a crisis in the housing model, exacerbated by the real estate bubble bursting in 2008 and subsequent economic downturn (DESCA 2020), a situation further aggravated by the COVID-19 pandemic.

However, beyond the issue of social exclusion—reflected in the concern of 83.6% of Spaniards who believe that not everyone has equal access to housing—the topic of squatting has increasingly become a focal point in recent years. Parties such as the PP, VOX, and, until its dissolution, Ciudadanos, alongside certain media outlets, "have perpetuated a narrative of exaggeration and manipulation around the phenomenon of squatting, turning it into a commonly accepted belief" (Cúneo 2020). Numerous reports indicate that what is often presented as a public safety crisis related to squatting actually pertains to cases of breaking and entering, not usurpation, since "they occupy empty apartments owned by banks and investment funds", rather than the appropriation of inhabited homes (Cúneo 2020).

In this context, respondents were asked to indicate their level of agreement with the statement: "The issue of squatting in Spain is minor and exaggerated by certain interests". The findings reveal that while 34.4% of respondents believe the issue is exaggerated, a substantial 65.6% disagree, viewing it as a more serious concern. Age appears to be a significant factor influencing responses, with younger respondents, particularly those aged 16 to 24, being more likely to consider squatting an exaggerated issue (48.5%), slightly less so among those aged 25 to 34 (40.5%). In contrast, only 27.1% of those over 65 share this view.

In a topic that has become a significant political issue, ideological alignment is crucial for understanding the level of agreement with the statement. Interestingly, the centre-right (18.1%) and the right (20.3%) are less inclined to view squatting as an exaggerated issue compared to the far right (24.6%). This suggests that more moderate conservative sectors are more supportive of the narrative surrounding the squatting issue.

Among the progressive groups, there is a gradual increase in the belief that the issue is exaggerated, from the left (43.2%) to the far left (56.9%), with centre-left views falling below the average (32.5%). Religious affiliation is once again significant when measuring agreement/disagreement, with two distinct positions emerging: while practising Catholics (76.7%) and non-practising Catholics (74.3%) are the most sceptical about the idea that squatting is an exaggerated issue, only 40.9% of those from other faiths and 48.1% of atheists share this scepticism.

When analysing by autonomous community, those most sceptical about the claim that squatting is an exaggerated issue include Castilla La Mancha (20.5%), Aragón (20.6%), and Extremadura (25.9%), which are not among the communities with the most squatting cases, whether categorised as usurpation or trespassing. In fact, according to data from the Ministry of Home Affairs, these were three of the communities that registered a decline in the first quarter of 2023 (Bustos 2023).

The Pandemic and Recognition of Sexual Diversity

Debate has persisted about the necessity of pandemic restrictions since the outbreak of COVID-19, especially considering the spread of disinformation (Salaverría et al. 2020; Aleixandre-Benavent et al. 2020) and conspiracy theories concerning lockdown measures (Palau-Sampio 2021a, b). In response, the survey asked whether "pandemic restrictions were a response to a unique health crisis rather than an attempt at control", which was supported by more than seven out of ten respondents, compared to 27.8% of respondents who disagreed with it. Although there are no significant age differences, support is notably higher among those aged 35 to 44 years (76.2%) and 55 to 64 years (77.2%), as well as residents of municipalities with populations between 200,000 and 500,000 inhabitants (77.1%).

Ideological affiliation also influenced responses, with those on the left (81.6%)—eight points above the average—and the far left (77.7%) showing higher levels of support, whereas only 49.1% of the far right agreed. Among those on the right, support was eight percentage points below the average (64.3%). These findings contrast with earlier projections made at the beginning of the pandemic, which indicated similar levels of support for different measures across all ideological groups (Miller 2020).

Religious beliefs also played a role, with declared atheists (81.2%) showing the highest level of agreement, compared to agnostics (68.5%). Similarly, educational attainment influenced perceptions; those with a master's degree or doctorate were most likely to agree (76.4%). Regionally, Asturias (92.3%), Murcia (84.6%), and the Basque Country (81.4%) exhibited the highest levels of agreement, whereas Aragón (64.7%) and Madrid (67.1%) showed lower levels of support.

Although agreement with the statement "recognition of sexual diversity (gay, lesbian, bisexual, and transgender) represents progress in human rights" is the highest (81.4%)—compared to 18.6% expressing disagreement—out of the seven statements made to measure ideological polarisation, the different variables reflect important nuances. Ideology, in particular, plays a critical role, with those on the left showing the strongest support (93.8%), while those on the far right are the least supportive (45.6%). This ideological divide aligns with the positions of political parties that represent these views (Carratalá 2021). While those identifying with the far left exceed the average level of agreement (84.6%), those on the right trail by 13 percentage points (68.1%). Religious beliefs also contribute to differing levels of agreement. Atheists (93.4%) and non-believers (87.8%) clearly support these views, whereas practising Catholics exhibit less agreement (72.9%).

Gender, as in the case of equality policies, shows clearer support from women (84.5%) than from men (78%). By age, support for the statement is above average across most age groups, except among those over 65 years old (76%). Castilla La Mancha (70.5%), Aragon (73.5%), and Castilla Leon (76.9%) are the communities that least support this statement, closely followed by Madrid (77.8%).

4.2 Disinformation

The dangers posed by disinformation to democratic coexistence (Bennett and Livingston 2018; Esser and Pfetsch 2020) have garnered such significant attention from international institutions (European Commission 2018; United Nations 2024) and governments (Funke and Flamini 2024), as well as within the academic community (Biloš 2019; Cea and Palomo 2021; López-García et al. 2021; López García 2023; Rúas Araújo and Paniagua Rojano 2023), that initiatives aimed at monitoring and mitigating its effects have been widely implemented. Disinformation is defined as "the deliberate creation and dissemination of false and/or manipulated information with the intent to deceive and mislead audiences, either for the purposes of causing harm, or for political, personal, or financial gain" (European Commission 2018). The initial warnings about its dangers became evident during the 2016 Brexit referendum (Cervi and Carrillo-Andrade 2019) and the 2016 US presidential campaign (Bovet and Makse 2019). Since then, its global impact has been widely documented, especially following the infodemic triggered by COVID-19 (Bechmann 2020; Zarocostas 2020).

Unlike misinformation, which involves the spread of false information due to error or professional malpractice, and malinformation, which involves the intentional release of truthful but ethically questionable content, disinformation is characterised by the deliberate manipulation of facts to create alternative realities (Lewandowsky et al. 2017). In an increasingly hybrid media environment, where traditional media coexist with social networks and pseudo-media (Palau-Sampio 2023), the potential for confusion has grown exponentially. The adulteration and falsification of images, data, photographs, or historical events not only undermine the principle of truthful information but also contribute to what is now referred to as the era of "information disorder" (Wardle and Derakhshan 2018), "disinformation order" (Bennett and Livingston 2018), or post-truth (Lewandowsky et al. 2017).

4.2 Disinformation

The phenomenon of disinformation has not gone unnoticed by the public. The Eurobarometer, a demographic study conducted by the European Union, reveals that 41% of Spaniards fully agree with the statement that "the existence of false news or information is a major issue" in Spain, with another 47% somewhat agreeing. These figures are 11 points higher than the EU average (77%). In this context, respondents highlighted disinformation as a significant threat to democracy: 87% of Spanish citizens and 81% of EU citizens share this concern. This widespread concern aligns with the high rates of false information detection, with four out of five Spanish citizens reporting frequent encounters with disinformation (12 points above the European average), and nearly six out of ten expressing confidence in their ability to detect such distorted content (Eurobarómetro 2023).

The phenomenon of disinformation is broad and multifaceted, challenging democratic norms and social cohesion (Palau-Sampio 2023). While digitalisation and social networks have democratised the power to spread disinformation and fuel global campaigns using bots and algorithms (Jungherr and Schroeder 2021), this issue is deeply intertwined with public communication processes and contemporary political polarisation. Rather than a straightforward cause-and-effect relationship where social media solely promotes disinformation, Tucker et al. (2018) describe a complex interaction where social media, political polarisation, and disinformation mutually reinforce each other in a self-perpetuating spiral, eroding democratic quality. Moreover, these three elements interact with other variables that amplify their impact, such as political engagement, the use of traditional media, and politicians' behaviours (Tucker et al. 2018).

Shu et al. (2020) highlight the considerable challenge of detecting disinformation: its varied forms, ranging from false texts to manipulated images and videos, with some content generated beyond human intervention (Shao et al. 2017).

The risks associated with disinformation are further exacerbated by structural issues, including a lack of trust in political and informational institutions (Bennett and Livingston 2023; Newman et al. 2024), which drive the consumption of information from non-mainstream sources (Fletcher and Park 2017; Jungherr and Schroeder 2021). Researchers also emphasise the challenge posed by the emotional component in combating disinformation, as individuals tend to perceive information as credible when it aligns with their existing beliefs and values (Scheufele and Krause 2019).

In the era of post-truth politics, where facts have less influence on shaping public opinion than pre-existing beliefs and values (Lockie 2017), the "elective affinity" fuelled by populist politics contributes to fragmentation and polarisation, turning public life into "a contest between rival versions of reality" (Waisbord 2018, p. 14). This is evident in the proliferation of extremist websites that promote disinformation and conspiracy theories, often linked to the far right (Van Prooijen et al. 2015; Haller and Holt 2019).

Research suggests that affective polarisation is shaped by the consumption of partisan and related information sources (Stroud 2010; Garrett et al. 2014; Lu and Lee 2019). This pattern, as previously discussed, leads users to engage with content that reinforces their existing viewpoints while avoiding exposure to opposing perspectives (Pariser 2011). These "echo chambers" or "filter bubbles" make detection and mitigation of disinformation particularly challenging (Qureshi et al. 2020).

The concern about disinformation has sparked a global fact-checking movement (Dias and Sippitt 2020) over the past three decades, now present in more than 100 countries (Stencel et al. 2023). While these platforms initially focused on political disinformation, their scope has expanded in response to the emergence of issues such as disinformation related to migration, gender, climate change, science, and health, particularly in the wake of the COVID-19 pandemic (Siwakoti et al. 2021).

As van Raemdonck and Meyer assert, "in the end disinformation is tackled first and foremost in citizens' attitudes and interactions with others" (2024, p. 18). This underscores the need to develop media literacy strategies, like those promoted by European and Spanish public institutions, which aim to equip citizens with the skills necessary to combat disinformation through a shared sense of responsibility (Sádaba and Salaverría 2023).

4.2.1 Perception of Disinformation in Spain

In Spain, disinformation is perceived as a significant issue, with 75.2% of the population considering it a "very important" issue, compared to nearly 20% who regard it as "just another issue" or "not very important" (Table 4.2). This concern, highlighted in the survey of 1200 people in Spain, is consistent with the findings of the *Eurobarometer* from autumn 2023 (Eurobarómetro 2023).

The survey results show that age plays a role in shaping perceptions of disinformation. Those over 55 years old are particularly concerned and categorise this issue as very relevant, exceeding the average by six percentage points. On the other hand, 25% of individuals under 35 tend to downplay the importance of disinformation. Ideological self-positioning is also a decisive factor. Those who identify as far-left (85.4%) or left (79.4%) are the most aware of the importance of the issue, while those who align themselves as centrist, right, or far-right tend to score it below the average.

Various studies have highlighted the importance of social networks as a vector for the spread of disinformation (Bradshaw and Howard 2018; Iosifidis and Nicoli 2020). This view is shared by many Spanish citizens. When asked to what extent the Internet and social networks have contributed to the spread of disinformation, 45.9% of respondents said that social networks have had a significant influence, a figure that is 13 percentage points higher than the 32.8% who attributed the same level of influence to the Internet (Table 4.3). Considering the timeline of these technologies, this suggests that social networks, which became popular in the first decade of the twenty-first century, are more strongly associated with the spread of disinformation than the Internet as a whole. However, it is noteworthy that one-third of respondents attribute some responsibility to the Internet, with 44.9% stating that its influence is "quite a bit".

4.2 Disinformation

Table 4.2 Degree of importance of disinformation in Spain (%)

| | Average | Ideological self-positioning | | | | | Age | | | | | |
		Far left	Left	Centre	Right	Far right	16–24	25–34	35–44	45–54	55–64	65+
A very significant issue	75.2	85.4	79.4	71.0	72.5	70.2	65.7	67.3	71.3	76.0	81.2	81.9
Just another issue	16.5	7.7	16.9	16.9	22.0	14.0	20.9	20.3	14.9	16.6	14.7	14.9
A minor issue	3.2	2.3	1.4	4.4	2.7	7.0	4.5	5.2	5.0	2.6	2.0	1.4
DNK	2.4	2.3	1.1	3.5	1.1	5.3	4.5	3.3	4.0	2.2	1.5	0.7
DNR	2.7	2.3	1.1	4.2	1.6	3.5	4.5	3.9	5.0	2.6	0.5	1.0

Table 4.3 Contribution of the Internet and social networks to disinformation (%)

	Internet	Social networks and influencers
A lot	32.8	45.9
Quite a bit	44.9	35.0
A little	13.5	11.1
None	3.9	3.4
DNK	2.7	3.0
DNR	2.2	1.7

Table 4.4 Sources of disinformation (%)

	Average	Gender		Ideological self-positioning				
		M	F	Far left	Left	Centre	Right	Far right
Social media	63.8	63.0	64.5	57.7	71.8	62.1	61.0	50.9
Traditional media in any format	25.9	24.2	27.4	32.3	25.4	25.2	23.1	28.1
Fake news websites	58.4	52.8	63.5	50.8	64.4	59.2	53.3	47.4
Political parties and their leaders	47.9	54.3	41.9	53.1	44.1	48.3	47.8	56.1
The government	28.1	32.0	24.5	13.1	11.3	32.7	47.3	66.7
Opposition parties	16.0	16.6	15.4	23.1	20.6	13.8	7.7	15.8
Foreign governments	5.2	5.2	5.1	3.8	4.2	6.3	6.0	1.8
Economic powers	30.2	29.1	31.2	45.4	35.9	25.4	25.3	15.8
Anti-system groups	13.9	14.4	13.4	6.2	10.2	16.5	19.2	15.8
Ordinary citizens	10.9	8.5	13.1	14.6	12.1	10.6	9.3	1.8

The survey revealed that perceptions of the Internet's role in disinformation are relatively consistent across different groups. In contrast, views on social networks and influencers show considerable variation depending on factors such as gender, age, and political self-identification. For instance, men tend to perceive a greater influence of social networks (50.3%) than women do, and this perception increases with age. While only 26.1% of those under 25 years of age rate this influence as "a lot", the percentage rises by 12 points in the next age group, reaching 56.3% among those over 65 years of age. Furthermore, political positioning also plays a role, with those identifying as left-wing (56.2%) or far-left (46.9%) perceiving a greater influence from social networks, significantly above the average.

4.2.1.1 Sources of Fake Content

When asked about the sources of disinformation, respondents primarily identified two: social media (63.8%) and fake news websites, the pseudo-media (58.4%) (Table 4.4). Following these were political parties and their leaders (47.8%), and three centres of power: economic (30.2%), political (government, 28.1%), and media (traditional or online, 25.9%). These findings highlight a significant detachment between citizens and institutions, including the media and government.

In the case of the media, one in four people not only distrusts them but also holds them responsible for actively spreading disinformation, indicating a significant challenge to how the media's work is perceived. At a second level, the source of disinformation is attributed to less influential political and social groups, such as opposition parties (16%), anti-system groups (13.9%), and ordinary citizens (10.9%). The influence of foreign governments is generally seen as minor, with only 5.2% of respondents considering them significant contributors to disinformation.

Perceptions of sources vary by gender, ideology, and age. For example, men are more likely to attribute responsibility to political parties (54.3%) and the government (32%), while women are more often inclined to blame pseudo-media (63.5%) and ordinary citizens (13.1%). Political self-positioning heavily influences the identification of sources of disinformation. The far right associates social networks (50.9%) and fake news websites (47.4%) as a source of disinformation much less—over 10 points below the average. This is consistent with the identification of pseudo-media associated with the far right in Spain (Palau-Sampio and Carratalá 2022), as well as with the social media activities of parties like VOX (Díez Garrido et al. 2021; Olmos Alcaraz 2023).

For the far right, however, the government is perceived as the primary source of disinformation (66.7%), a perception that is almost six times higher than among left-wing (13.1%) and far-left (11.3%) voters. The right wing also views the government as a significant source, their perception being almost twice the average. This focus on the government as a source of disinformation is directly related to the ideological distance from the ruling coalition at the time of the survey in March 2023, which was formed by the Socialist Party and Unidas Podemos. In contrast, left-wing and far-left respondents place three times more responsibility on opposition parties than the right does (7.7%). Both extremes of the political spectrum agree by more than the average that political parties and their leaders play a significant role in spreading disinformation.

Compared to previous results, left-wing voters are more inclined to blame social networks (71.8%) and pseudo-media (64.4%), with these figures being 14 points higher than those among the far left. The far left, however, views economic powers as major sources of disinformation (45.4%), a perception largely shared by the left (35.9%). In contrast, only 15.8% of far-right respondents believe that these economic powers are potential propagators of false content, the same percentage that attributes this responsibility to anti-system groups. For the far left, the disinformation potential of these groups (6.2%) is much lower than that of ordinary citizens (14.6%), whom the far right sees as playing an insignificant role (1.8%).

The generational factor also significantly influences when identifying sources of disinformation specifically for three actors: economic powers, political parties and their leaders, and traditional media. Younger respondents, especially those under 25, are less likely to view economic powers as a threat (17.2%), while this perception doubles among older generations. A similar trend is observed with political parties and leaders, with a gradual increase in their association as a source of disinformation from the 25–34 age group (35.3%) to the older group (57.6%). Interestingly, the 16 to 24 age group exhibits a notable distrust of traditional media, attributing a similar level of potential for disinformation to them as political parties (41.8%), placing them third behind social networks and pseudo-media.

Table 4.5 Degree of disinformation originating in different areas (%)

Assessment	Social networks	Politics	Advertising and marketing	Media	Business and economic sector
A lot	55.9	52.0	28.3	21.4	18.4
Quite a bit	34.1	37.7	49.0	53.8	48.5
A little	7.1	7.6	19.2	21.9	30.3
None	2.9	2.7	3.5	2.9	2.7

When assessing the degree of disinformation generated across different areas, both social networks and politics emerge as the most significant, with very similar percentages (Table 4.5). Nine out of ten respondents believe that these two areas are responsible for a lot, or quite a bit, of disinformation. Notably, the majority of those surveyed indicated that social networks generate "a lot" of disinformation (55.9%), followed closely by politics (52%). Although to a lesser extent, respondents also attributed responsibility for disinformation to advertising and marketing (77.3%) and the media (75.2%), reflecting a generally low level of trust in these sectors compared to persuasive communication strategies.

Despite the stakes involved, the business and economic sector scored eight points lower (66.9%). However, there are notable differences when considering the degree of disinformation perceived in the political sphere: 68.4% of those who identify with the far right believe that politics generates "a lot" of disinformation—16 points higher than the average. Gender also plays a role, with men more likely to assess the level of disinformation in politics as "a lot" (57.8%) compared to women (46.7%).

4.2.1.2 Combatting Disinformation

Three-quarters of the respondents believe that public authorities should take action to combat disinformation, compared to 8.8% who do not (Table 4.6). Support for these interventions is particularly strong among those over 55 years old and individuals who identify with the far left (86.9%) and left (83.3%), exceeding the far right (66.6%) by almost 20 points. This suggests that those with more left-leaning views advocate government intervention to tackle disinformation, while those with more conservative views are less enthusiastic.

When asked about possible measures to combat disinformation, the majority favoured economic sanctions over more drastic actions like shutting down broadcasts. Only 13.8% supported banning future publications, whereas nearly three times as many (36.3%) preferred financial penalties (Table 4.7). Women, in particular, were more likely to support economic sanctions (40.4%), as well as those in the 25 to 34 age group.

Among the four proposed options, the second most popular was educational in nature, with one in four respondents advocating for measures aimed at training citizens to identify disinformation, with no significant differences in gender or age, but stronger support among those with higher education (30.4%). Additionally, 19.5%

4.2 Disinformation

Table 4.6 Should public authorities take action against disinformation? (%)

	Average	Ideological self-positioning					Age					
		Far left	Left	Centre	Right	Far right	16–24	25–34	35–44	45–54	55–64	65+
Yes	77.1	86.9	83.3	72.1	74.7	66.7	67.9	68.0	67.8	79.0	86.3	85.1
No	8.8	5.4	4.2	10.8	12.6	15.8	12.7	12.4	9.4	7.0	6.6	7.6
DNK	10.3	5.4	11.0	11.9	8.2	10.5	16.4	14.4	16.3	10.0	5.1	4.9
DNR	3.7	2.3	1.4	5.2	4.4	7.0	3.0	5.2	6.4	3.9	2.0	2.4

Table 4.7 Preferred actions against disinformation (%)

	Average	Ideological self-positioning				
		Far left	Left	Centre	Right	Far right
Closing broadcasts or banning future publications	13.8	9.7	13.6	12.1	19.1	23.7
Economic sanctions for those who publish disinformation	36.3	31.9	34.9	38.7	35.3	42.1
Creation of a state body or specific courts	19.5	22.1	22.4	17.9	16.2	15.8
Training citizens to identify disinformation	24.8	31.9	26.1	22.8	23.5	15.8
DNK	5.6	4.4	3.1	8.4	5.9	2.6

of respondents supported the creation of a state body or specific courts to address cases of disinformation, with men (23.8%) and respondents older than 65 showing the most support for this legal approach.

Ideological self-positioning played a significant role in shaping opinions on the various measures. In this regard, left-leaning positions tend to favour more social and institutional measures, such as citizen training—which the far left supports on par with economic sanctions, with 31.9% backing—or the creation of specific bodies. On the opposite end, the far right leans towards more forceful options: 42.1% of the far right supports economic fines, and 23.7% back the prohibition of broadcasts as actions against disinformation, with these figures being seven and four percentage points higher, respectively, than those expressed by the right-wing population. Support for broadcast closures is also higher among those with less than university-level education (18.6% among those with primary education and 17.4% with secondary education), nearly double the responses from those with university degrees (9.8%) or master's and doctoral degrees (9.0%).

4.2.1.3 Detection and Action by Citizens

According to the Interactive Advertising Bureau's 2023 data, in Spain, of the 37.8 million people aged 12 to 74, 94% are Internet users, and 85% use social media (IAB 2023). The survey of those over 16 years old found that nearly eight out of ten respondents use some form of social media or messaging service, such as X (formerly Twitter), Facebook, Instagram, or WhatsApp, to obtain information, while 21.8% said they do not use these platforms (IAB 2023). The survey highlights that 69.1% of those who use social media or messaging services have detected some form of disinformation, a figure five times higher than those who have not (13.6%) (Table 4.8). A total of 17.3% of respondents didn't know or didn't respond.

Gender, age, and educational level were found to be the most relevant factors in detecting disinformation. In fact, men (74.9%) are more likely to identify disinformation than women (63.7%). This likelihood increases with age, from 62.7% among those aged 16 to 24 to 72.9% among those over 65. Similarly, detection rates rise with educational level: from 42.9% among those with less than primary education

4.2 Disinformation

Table 4.8 Detection of disinformation on social media or messaging apps (%)

	Average	Gender		Level of education					
		M	F	Less than primary education	Primary education	Intermediate studies	University graduate	Master's and PhD	DNK/DNR
Yes	69.1	74.9	63.7	42.9	52.3	70.3	70.9	77.7	25.0
No	13.6	10.4	16.6	42.9	21.5	14.2	12.7	8.8	–
DNK	12.9	10.6	15.0	14.3	20.6	10.8	14.3	9.5	18.8
DNR	4.4	4.2	4.6	–	5.6	4.6	2.1	4.1	56.3

Table 4.9 Comparison between consumption and identified disinformation (%)

	Average consumption	Average disinformation detected
X	25.9	33.1
Facebook	45.1	59.6
Instagram	35.3	30.9
TikTok	13.7	15.9
WhatsApp	46.1	45.6
Twitch	4.0	3.7
YouTube	36.1	21.1
Telegram	14.5	7.2
Email	–	0.6
Google news	0.5	–
LinkedIn	0.2	–
Other	0.5	1.2
DNK/DNR	21.8	0.5

to 77.7% among those with a master's or doctoral degree. The size of the population where one lives also influences the results, with 77.9% detection among those living in towns with more than 500,000 inhabitants, compared to 66.3% in municipalities with fewer than 10,000 inhabitants. Ideological self-positioning shows that voters on the left (75.7%) and the right (71.4%) are more likely to detect disinformation on social media and messaging apps.

The survey reveals that the social network where disinformation is most frequently detected is Facebook, according to six out of ten respondents (Table 4.9). Although Facebook is the second most used platform for information (45.1%), the proportion of respondents identifying disinformation on it exceeds this percentage by almost 15 points. With the exception of the 16 to 24 age group (33.3%), which also uses it the least (21%), the rest of the age groups show values close to the average (see also Fig. 4.2).

The second most mentioned platform for detected disinformation is X, identified by 33.1% of respondents, despite being the fourth most used platform (25.9%). This is followed by Instagram (30.9%), which is used by 35.2% of people, and YouTube (21.1%), which is used by 36.1% for information. On TikTok, the percentage of disinformation identified (15.9%) exceeds the number of users by two points, and

Fig. 4.2 Comparison between the use of social networks and messaging apps and the detection of disinformation by age group (%)

4.2 Disinformation

Table 4.10 On which social networks or messaging apps have you detected disinformation? By gender and ideology (%)

	Gender		Ideological self-positioning				
	M	F	Far left	Left	Centre	Right	Far right
X	37.6	28.1	45.5	33.6	31.5	28.5	30.0
Facebook	58.9	60.3	61.4	58.2	62.3	53.8	62.5
Instagram	26.8	35.4	35.2	31.0	30.2	30.8	27.5
TikTok	16.6	15.1	22.7	13.4	15.1	18.5	15.0
WhatsApp	50.3	40.5	52.3	48.1	46.9	37.7	30.0
Twitch	4.8	2.5	6.8	2.2	4.6	3.1	2.5
YouTube	25.2	16.6	25.0	22.8	19.3	18.5	22.5
Telegram	8.1	6.3	8.0	7.5	7.9	6.2	2.5
Email	0.7	0.5	1.1	–	0.7	1.5	–
Other	1.4	1.0	–	0.7	2.0	0.8	2.5
DNK/DNR	0.5	0.5	–	1.1	–	0.8	–

on Twitch it is slightly lower than that usage rate (4%). When analysing by gender, men are more likely to notice disinformation on X and YouTube, while women detect it more on Instagram, which aligns with their higher usage rates of these platforms.

In the case of the two messaging apps included in the survey, WhatsApp and Telegram, the results were mixed. WhatsApp is not only more widely used (46.1%) but is also the second most reported source of disinformation after Facebook. The percentage of men who use WhatsApp (50.5%) and identify disinformation on it (50.3%) is proportionate, as is the case with women (41.9% usage and 40.5% detection). Telegram, used by 14.5% of respondents as a source of information, is cited by half of them as a source of disinformation (7.2%).

Unlike applications such as WhatsApp, which have a relatively balanced presence across generations, the use of most social networks varies depending on age group. Among younger users, platforms like TikTok, Instagram, and Twitch are more prevalent, while older users tend to prefer Facebook. The intermediate age groups are more likely to use platforms like YouTube, X, and Telegram (IAB 2023). Given these generational differences, the survey compared reported usage by age group with the detection of disinformation across six social networks and two messaging apps.

The ideological factor is shown to influence the perception of disinformation, particularly among those who identify with the far left. Except for Facebook, respondents who identify as far left tend to report higher levels of disinformation across all six social networks and two messaging apps (Table 4.10). For example, 52.3% of far-left respondents identified disinformation on WhatsApp, a difference of more than 20 points compared to the far right, where only 30% identified disinformation. For X, the gap is 15 points. The difference narrows on platforms like Instagram and TikTok, where the gap between the far left and far right is seven points. Higher levels of education, such as university studies or master's and

Table 4.11 Reaction to detection of fake news on social media or messaging apps (%)

	Average	Ideological self-positioning					Age					
		Far left	Left	Centre	Right	Far right	16–24	25–34	35–44	45–54	55–64	65+
Verify authenticity via fact-checker	34.7	36.2	35.6	34.8	33.5	28.1	38.8	33.3	36.6	29.7	37.1	34.4
Verify through traditional media	43.1	34.6	47.5	41.3	46.2	42.1	41.8	39.9	46.0	46.7	43.7	40.3
Report the content as false	24.7	33.8	22.9	24.8	20.3	28.1	29.1	26.8	28.7	19.7	25.4	22.2
Notify someone if I shared it	13.9	14.6	15.8	12.9	12.1	14.0	13.4	17.6	11.4	8.7	14.2	17.7
Stop following the person or source	22.7	26.9	20.3	21.5	25.8	28.1	14.2	22.2	18.3	26.6	23.9	26.0

4.2 Disinformation

Table 4.12 Reactions to content you like or dislike on social media (%)

	Reaction to content you like		Reaction to content you dislike
Share with others	20.7	Share with others	0.5
Give it a "like"	33.3	Give it a negative reaction	9.3
Comment on it	9.2	Comment on it	3.2
Do nothing	36.8	Do nothing	87.1

doctoral degrees, also correlate with higher detection rates of disinformation on all platforms—except Facebook and TikTok—compared to those with primary and secondary education.

When respondents detect possible fake news on social media, most choose to verify the content through the media (Table 4.11). This approach, selected by four out of ten respondents, demonstrates a continued trust in traditional media as a reliable source of information. This method is also favoured by the youngest group, aged 16 to 24 (41.8%), even though they consider the media to be the third most significant channel for spreading false content. On the other hand, those identifying as far-left are more reluctant to do this, almost 10 points below the average.

The second most common option for verifying content is using a fact-checking platform, chosen by 34.7% of respondents. This alternative is more favoured by left-wing voters, while far-right voters rank it as a secondary option. Among the other possible reactions, 24.7% of respondents said they would report the content as false, 22.7% would stop following the source, and 13.9% would inform their contacts if they had shared the disinformation.

One of the main methods by which disinformation spreads is the viral sharing of messages among users, a practice that was notably highlighted during the COVID-19 pandemic (Sánchez-Duarte and Rosa 2020). For this reason, respondents were asked what type of content they usually interact with or choose to share based on their preferences. When users encounter content they find relevant, 63.2% said they would give it a "like" or a similar form of acknowledgement. A third of respondents share such content with others (21.7%), while a smaller proportion leaves comments (9.2%) (Table 4.12). However, 36.8% of respondents said they do not engage in these circumstances.

The likelihood of interacting with content drastically drops when users encounter information they dislike through social networks. In these cases, 87% of respondents said they "do nothing". Only 9.3% react negatively to the content, and 3.2% leave a comment. Moreover, only 0.5% would share content they dislike with others.

Although there are no differences between genders in the reactions, generational differences stand out in two key areas. First, younger respondents, especially those aged 16 to 24, are more likely to interact with content, whether by giving a like (47.8%) or a dislike (12.8%), especially when compared to those aged 54 to 65, who score 26.4% and 7.4%. However, this older group is the most likely to comment on whether they like (10.7%) or dislike (4.9%) content. People over 65 years old are

Table 4.13 Actions taken before sharing content (%)

Only reading the headline	3.8
Reading the headline and checking the source	13.8
Reading the headline, checking the source, and reading the text	79.9
None of the above	2.5

more inclined to share content (23.4%) compared to those under 25 (14.2%), and they are also the only group that shares content they don't like (2%).

Ideological self-positioning influences some of the respondents' actions. The extremes of the political spectrum show different behaviours when it comes to sharing content they like: while those on the far left do so less than the average (16.9%), those on the far right (33.3%) share content twice as much. Both groups are the most active in commenting on content they both agree with and disagree with. The far left tends to be more active in expressing negative reactions to content they don't like (13.6%), while the far right does so to a lesser extent (7.7%).

A key aspect of evaluating the viral spread of disinformation is understanding under what conditions the content is shared. To address this, respondents were asked what precautions they take before sharing content. Eight out of ten respondents said they meet three prerequisites: having read the headline, checking the source, and reading the text (Table 4.13). An additional 13.8% reported following two of these steps. However, 3.8% admitted to sharing content after only reading the headline, and 2.5% acknowledged sharing without any of the aforementioned precautions.

Age proves to be a determining factor in impulsiveness: those under 25 years old are twice as likely as the average to share content without reading anything (5.3%) or after only reading the headline (8.4%), and they have the lowest rates (70.5%) for sharing after "reading the headline, checking the source, and reading the text". People with a master's or doctoral degree show the highest levels of responsibility before sharing content (84.8%), while those who identify with the far left are the most diligent in following all three steps before sharing (88.4%), compared to 70.5% of those on the far right. Notably, 11.4% of people who identify with the far right share content without reading anything or just the headline.

Open Access This chapter is licensed under the terms of the Creative Commons Attribution 4.0 International License (http://creativecommons.org/licenses/by/4.0/), which permits use, sharing, adaptation, distribution and reproduction in any medium or format, as long as you give appropriate credit to the original author(s) and the source, provide a link to the Creative Commons license and indicate if changes were made.

The images or other third party material in this chapter are included in the chapter's Creative Commons license, unless indicated otherwise in a credit line to the material. If material is not included in the chapter's Creative Commons license and your intended use is not permitted by statutory regulation or exceeds the permitted use, you will need to obtain permission directly from the copyright holder.

Chapter 5
Information Consumption and Trust

Exploring the factors that explain why audiences choose certain content or connect with specific media has been a central theme in mass communication research since its beginnings (McQuail 1994; Ruggiero 2000). Since the 1970s, the uses and gratifications theory has gained prominence, particularly through the work of Katz et al. (1973). This theory examines not only the gratifications sought by audiences but also how they use media to satisfy social and psychological needs (Ruggiero 2000). According to this approach, audiences actively select from various options based on the media's ability to meet different needs, such as information, entertainment, social interaction, or escape (Katz et al. 1973, 1999; Ruggiero 2000).

Over the past few decades, the uses and gratifications theory has focused on different media and their capacity to fulfil specific demands, associating the press with the need for information and television with the need for entertainment (Diddi and LaRose 2006). However, the advent of the Internet (Papacharissi and Rubin 2000) and social media, along with the associated consumption patterns, has exponentially broadened analytical perspectives. These range from the complementarity between traditional and digital media (Dutta-Bergman 2004) to the factors influencing their substitution, such as habits, accessibility, or usability (van der Wurff 2011; Dimmick et al. 2004; Boczkowski et al. 2018). Other considerations include credibility, quality, representativeness (Sundar 1999), type of content, scope of coverage, or formats (van der Wurff 2011).

The way citizens access information has changed dramatically over the last two decades, amid intense technological transformations, an overabundance of information, and a loss of trust in traditional media. Various studies have highlighted the growing gap between these factors, which has serious implications for democratic coexistence and the sustainability of the media itself, as trust becomes a predictor of the willingness to pay for information (Schibsted 2024). In Spain, the percentage of people subscribing to newspapers has remained below 12% in recent years, significantly lower than in countries like Norway (40%) and Sweden (31%) (Newman et al. 2024).

5.1 Credibility Crisis and Access to News

The evolution in access to and consumption of news in a hybrid media context (Chadwick 2013) has revealed a significant gap between the media agenda and the public's information preferences (Boczkowski and Mitchelstein 2015), which tends to be more interested in soft content, such as sports, events, and entertainment, rather than issues of political and social relevance (Reinemann et al. 2012). In Spain, these trends are evident in the disparities between the media's agenda and the interests of its web audience, who are more attracted to soft news and clickbait techniques (Diez-Gracia and Sánchez-García 2022). However, the popularity of such news rarely translates into genuine user satisfaction (Groot Kormelink and Meijer 2018; Costera Meijer 2021).

Compounding this disconnect in the ability to focus the audience's attention on important topics is the trend of obtaining information through online channels. The Reuters Institute reports that nearly half of the Spanish population uses social media as their primary source of information, with 72% getting their news online (Newman et al. 2024).

This type of online consumption has been associated with two trends. First, there is a more informal, fragmented, and occasional consumption of news, mediated by technology, as illustrated by the article written by Boczkowski et al. (2018): "News comes across when I'm in a moment of leisure". Second, the phenomenon of "News Finds Me", where individuals feel they do not need to actively search for content to stay informed because relevant news will reach them through their social media (Gil de Zúñiga et al. 2017).

In recent years, another phenomenon influencing news consumption or avoidance has been what is known as information fatigue, caused by an overabundance of information and overexposure, often to negative news. The Reuters Institute report for Spain indicates that 44% of the Spanish population experiences information fatigue (Labiano-Juangarcía et al. 2024). Although the decline in interest in news has stabilised—from 82% to 53% between 2015 and 2023—Spain has seen one of the most significant increases in news fatigue, rising from 26% in 2019 to 44% in 2024 (Newman et al. 2024). As a result of this fatigue, 37% of the Spanish population admits to actively avoiding the news, with a higher incidence among young people and those who use social media for information (Labiano-Juangarcía et al. 2024). The percentage of individuals who avoid the news has increased by eight percentage points compared to the previous year (Newman et al. 2024).

The use of social media as the main source of information has been linked to low trust in mainstream media (Tsfati 2010; Fletcher and Park 2017; Kalogeropoulos et al. 2019). Various studies have highlighted a worrying trend in recent years, especially in the Spanish context. Data from the Digital News Report Spain 2024 reveal that 39% of Spaniards distrust the news (Labiano-Juangarcía et al. 2024). Moreover, among those under 25 years of age, this figure reaches 56%, compared to 19% who express trust. These findings are consistent with the results from the 2023 Trust

Barometer, which showed that trust in the media in Spain (38%) is significantly below the global average (50%) (Edelman 2023).

At the European level, the Eurobarometer survey from January 2023 indicates that only 27% of Spaniards trust the media—European average: 38% (European Commission 2023)—compared to 70% who do not. The Social Trends Survey conducted by the Sociological Research Centre (CIS) also highlights a loss of trust among Spanish citizens in traditional media. On a scale of 1 to 10, respondents rated this trust at 4.1, two-tenths lower than in the previous 2 years (CIS 2023).

What are the keys to trust in information? Based on a large-scale citizen survey, The Trust Project identified eight key indicators of trust in news: transparency, specialisation, identification of genre type, sources, work process, proximity and knowledge, diversity of voices, and promoting interactivity with audiences (The Trust Project 2024).

5.2 Degree of Information and Preferences

According to a survey of 1200 people, carried out within the CIAICO2021/125 research project, Spaniards generally express a high level of satisfaction with the amount of information they have on topics that interest them. Three out of four respondents (76.2%) rate their knowledge of current events positively, while 17.6% consider it inadequate. Additionally, nearly half (46.6%) believe their level of information has improved compared to previous years, with a similar percentage (43.1%) indicating no change in their information levels. Women, in particular, are more confident that the amount of information they receive has improved in recent years.

The phenomenon of news avoidance highlights the importance of exploring which types of content generate greater rejection. The most frequently avoided content by respondents includes that with excessive advertising (69.1%), a figure that is more than double the second most cited reason for avoidance: overly lengthy information (32.4%). Respondents who identify as left wing are the most critical of advertising (74.9%), while those on the right tend to avoid extensive content more (41.8%).

The survey also indicates a preference for brief and visual information among the 16 to 24 age group, who are less bothered by advertising (61.9%). This group is more likely to avoid information without images (12.7% compared to an average of 8.3%), while those aged 25 to 34 are least tolerant of information that only contains video (23.5% compared to an average of 15.2%). Notably, 17.5% of Spaniards state that they do not avoid any specific type of content.

Various studies have shown that the sociodemographic characteristics of the audience influence the type of information consumed. Factors such as gender and age (Boulianne and Shehata 2022), educational level, and the audience's interest in politics (Strömbäck et al. 2013) are significant in determining different patterns of information consumption. The element of proximity, beyond representing news value (Shoemaker et al. 2007), also acts as a conditioning factor in media attention

(Gebremeskel and de Vries 2015). Additionally, the effects of affective or ideological polarisation can influence selective exposure to certain content while leading to the avoidance of others that may cause cognitive dissonance (Iyengar and Hahn 2009).

5.2.1 Proximity Information

Local issues are the primary information preference for nearly half of Spaniards (48.7%), almost 20 points ahead of national news (28.5%) (Table 5.1). The prioritisation order indicates that proximity is a significant factor in how people choose to inform themselves. Indeed, when respondents identified their second area of interest, regional news was most commonly selected, with four out of ten choosing it, followed by national news (25.4%).

Although national news generates the most overall interest when considering all three choices (89%), it only ranks first in the third option (35.1%), surpassing other areas at this point. Local news (78.4%) and regional news (74.4%) rank second and third, respectively. International news is relevant to 42.2% of Spaniards.

An analysis of the primary focus of each area reveals some differences for age and gender. Local news is more appealing to individuals aged 25 to 54, while only 36.6% of those 24 or younger show interest. Conversely, the youngest group has twice the average interest in international news (15.7%). National news is most relevant to those over 65 years of age (39.9%), while regional news is more evenly distributed across age groups. Generally, women prefer local news (53.9% compared to 43.1% of men), while men prefer national news (34.4% compared to 23% of women) and, to a lesser extent, international news (8.8% compared to 5.6% of women).

By region, Aragón (73.5%) and Navarre (72.2%) have the highest interest in local news, while Asturias (30.8%) and Cantabria (26.7%) show a preference for regional news. Madrid leads in preference for national coverage (46.1%), followed by the Valencian Community (38.8%), which also shows the second least interest in local news.

Political orientation reveals a greater attraction to national issues among the far right (42.1%), compared to the left (55.1%) and right (51.6%), who show more

Table 5.1 Most preferred information topics (%)

	Local	Regional	National	International
First	48.7	10.3	28.5	7.1
Second	13.3	41.4	25.4	14.5
Third	16.4	22.7	35.1	20.5
DNK/no order	21.6	25.6	11.0	57.8
Average	78.4	74.4	89.0	42.2

5.2 Degree of Information and Preferences

interest in local news. The far left places more importance on regional (13.8%) and international (10.0%) issues.

Educational level influences preferences, with those with lower education levels showing a clearer preference for local news, while those with university degrees prefer national news, and those with master's or doctoral degrees lean more towards international news. Smaller communities (fewer than 10,000 inhabitants) show a slight preference for local news (52.3%).

5.2.2 Relevant Topics

According to the survey of 1200 people, hard news is the main information interest for Spaniards. Health tops the list of concerns for nearly half of the population (46.1%), with a clear emphasis among women (Table 5.2). The economy (38%) follows as the second area of interest, with politics (33.9%) also significant. In both cases, men's interest is 18 points higher than women's or double it, particularly in political information.

A secondary block of attention includes various social interest topics, such as culture (28.1%), education (28.3%), and science and technology (28.3%). In all three areas, gender influences preferences: women show more interest in education (38.6%) and culture (34.6%), while men are more interested in science and technology (35.5%).

Although the environment is relevant to nearly one in five people (19.8%), this topic ranks lower than social life and current affairs (24.1%) or sports (22.8%) on the Spanish agenda. Gender does not significantly affect interest in environmental issues; however, it is a key factor in sports (36.7% for men and 9.9% for women) and social life and current affairs, where women's interest (30.2%) nearly doubles

Table 5.2 Topics of most interest to stay informed (%)

	Average	M	F	Ideological self-positioning				
				Far left	Left	Centre	Right	Far right
Politics	33.9	45.8	22.9	46.2	34.2	25.0	42.9	50.9
Economy	38.0	47.6	29.1	30.0	33.1	40.4	45.6	42.1
Sports	22.8	36.7	9.9	19.2	23.2	21.9	25.3	28.1
Environment	19.8	18.7	20.8	22.3	25.1	18.1	15.4	8.8
Health	46.1	36.7	54.9	46.2	44.4	47.9	43.4	50.9
Education	28.3	17.1	38.6	26.9	25.4	31.9	26.9	22.8
Science and technology	28.1	35.5	21.3	25.4	32.8	28.7	23.6	14.0
Culture	28.8	22.7	34.6	33.1	36.7	25.0	22.5	22.8
Social life, current affairs, etc.	24.1	17.5	30.2	16.9	22.9	24.8	29.7	24.6
Gender equality	7.1	2.9	10.9	15.4	8.5	5.4	3.3	5.3
Others	3.3	2.8	3.8	6.2	3.4	2.3	4.4	1.8
No interest in staying informed	2.0	1.4	2.6	0.8	0.8	3.3	1.6	1.8

that of men. Gender equality is of minor interest (7.1%) and is almost irrelevant to men (2.9%).

Some topics are clearly influenced by ideological alignment, while others, like health, are more universal, though it garners the most attention among the far right (50.9%). Politics interests the extremes (50.9% far right and 46.2% left) more than the centre (25%). This alignment is evident in topics such as gender equality, where interest from the far left (15.4%) is three times that of the right (5.3%), or in sports, where the far right is the most interested (28.1%) and the far left shows the least interest (19.2%).

The left has a stronger interest in science and technology (32.8%), culture (36.7%), and the environment (25.1%), while the right is more interested in the economy (45.6%) and social life and current affairs (29.7%). The centre tends to focus more on education (31.9%). In terms of location, politics (40.4%) and the economy (43.8%) are of more interest to residents of cities with more than half a million inhabitants, whereas the environment (26.6%) and education (34.2%) are more popular in towns with fewer than 10,000 people.

By age, the primary topics of interest for those over 54 are health, politics, and the economy. Among the younger population, science and technology (40.4%), social life and current affairs (36.6%), and sports (31.3%) are the standout issues. For those aged 25 to 34, culture (41.8%) is the top priority, while education is the main focus for those aged 35 to 44 (40.6%).

5.2.3 Media Type

The media serve various communicative purposes. Respondents' engagement with information sources varies based on three parameters: habitual consumption, seeking in-depth information on certain news topics, and evaluating media based on quality and the provision of well-verified news.

The results indicate that live or on-demand television is the primary source of information for two-thirds of respondents (64.8%), followed by social media (49.9%), digital newspapers (44.5%), live radio or podcasts (36.5%), and traditional newspapers in print or online (36.3%). The strong presence of social media in the information diet is underscored by the fact that 47.4% of respondents—61.9% of those aged 16 to 24—believe they can stay well-informed without following traditional media, compared to 42.5% who think "it is necessary to get information through traditional media". This belief is more common among those over 45 (from 47.2% to 53.5%) and those with far-right political views (54.4%).

Thirty-four is the age that marks a distinct divide in the consumption of television and social media as information sources. While television use falls below 50%, the use of social media as the main source reaches 76% among the youngest and 68.6% among those aged 25 to 34. By ideological affiliation, television is more popular among the right (70.9%) and far right (70.2%), while digital newspapers are more prevalent among the far left (48.5%) and left (52.0%). A similar pattern is

5.2 Degree of Information and Preferences

observed with educational levels: individuals with a master's or doctorate prefer social media as their primary source of information (56.8%), ranking television third (47.3%), after digital newspapers (56.1%).

Interestingly, the three most-consumed media types have a lower percentage of perceived quality than their usage rates. The gap between consumption and quality perception is more than 10 points for television (53.2%) and nearly 20 for social media (31.9%). In contrast, digital newspapers show a smaller gap of three percentage points (41.6%). Live radio or podcasts (48.2%) and traditional newspapers in print or online (45.1%) are rated nearly 10 percentage points higher than average consumption.

The third criterion considered—what medium is used to obtain in-depth information about certain news items—reveals patterns that diverge from the previous two approaches: search engines are now the most prominently used medium. Nearly half of the respondents use search engines, well ahead of television (33.7%), social media (29.8%), or digital newspapers (29.3%). Traditional newspapers in print or online (21.5%) and live radio or podcasts (19%) are less commonly used for this purpose (Table 5.3).

Those who seek in-depth information through Internet searches are typically aged 25 to 54 (from 56.9% to 53.3%), hold master's or doctoral degrees (58.1%), identify as left wing (57.1%), and describe themselves as agnostic (58.9%) or atheist (56.4%).

The survey enquired about the media sources respondents use to obtain information, including television, radio, and print. For television, the results only partially align with the 2023 audience rankings, where *Antena 3* leads (Zárate 2023).

Table 5.3 Comparison between media used (%)

Commonly used media to obtain information	Assessment	Media used to obtain in-depth information about certain news items	Assessment	Media offering high quality or more reliable information	Assessment
Live or on-demand television	64.8	Live or on-demand television	33.7	Live or on-demand television	53.2
Live radio or podcast	36.5	Live radio or podcast	19.0	Live radio or podcast	48.2
Traditional newspapers (print or online)	36.3	Traditional newspapers (print or online)	21.5	Traditional newspapers (print or online)	45.1
Digital newspapers	44.5	Digital newspapers	29.3	Digital newspapers	41.6
Social media	49.9	Social media	29.8	Other traditional digital media	18.0
Others	5.0	Search using search engines	48.5	Social media	31.9
		Others	3.6	Others	12.4
				None	16.5

However, they provide insights into the audience demographics for each medium. For *Antena 3*, the audience profile is predominantly right wing (75.2%) and far right (72.5%), with the under-25 age group being the most prominent (Table 5.4). Telecinco also attracts a larger audience under 45, particularly those aged 16 to 24 (36.7%). Both networks have a higher female audience: 57.5% on *Antena 3* and 28.1% on Telecinco. At Telecinco, the most significant group of viewers identifies as far right (27.5%), though the audience is broadly balanced ideologically.

The second most-watched channel among respondents is TVE, with a predominantly male audience (55.3%) and a majority identifying as left wing (57.3%). The 55–64 age group is particularly represented (52.8%), though the distribution does not indicate a significant generational gap, similar to La Sexta. The third most-followed channel among those surveyed (29.2%) is La Sexta, which has an audience largely self-identified as left wing (41.8%) and far left (40.3%), with the latter group being three times more numerous than their right-wing counterparts.

The survey results for radio stations align partially with the third wave of the EGM for 2023 (EGM 2023) (Estudio General de Medios refers to a periodic study conducted in Spain to measure media audiences, including television, radio, and digital platforms), except for *Cadena Ser*, which leads in both cases. The *Prisa* group station does not show a clear generational profile among its listeners, highlighting two groups: ages 25 to 34 (53.6%) and 55 to 64 (60.3%). However, it does exhibit a strong ideological profile, with a significant following among the far left (77.8%) and left (71.4%), tripling the representation compared to their political opposites.

COPE and *Onda Cero* are tied as the second choice among respondents. *COPE* has a notable far right following (77.8%), 10 times the far left's (7.4%). *Onda Cero*, with a more moderate profile, has a majority of listeners on the right (50%) and far right (44%), while *Radio Nacional* is predominantly followed by the left (49.6%). The public station shows a uniform age distribution, unlike *COPE*, which has its largest group of followers aged 16 to 24 (46.7%), and *Onda Cero*, which appeals most to those aged 45 to 54 (37.6%).

For the four selected newspapers, the survey's average follow-up matches the audience results (AIMC 2023). *El País*, leading the ranking, has a progressive reader profile (85% far left and 82.7% left), with lower representation among those aged 16 to 24, contrasting with *El Mundo*, *ABC*, and *La Razón*, which have their highest percentage of readers in this age group. Ideologically, *El Mundo* attracts a centre (53.3%) and right wing (57.1%) audience, while *ABC* appeals to the right (42.9%) and *La Razón* the far right (26.7%).

Among the four selected digital newspapers, the most consumed by respondents is eldiario.es, followed by *El Confidencial*, *OK Diario*, and *El Español*, a ranking that does not concur with the audience figures (Invertia 2024). Ideological self-positioning shows a left (51.6%) and far left (49.9%) alignment for eldiario.es, while *OK Diario* has a majority of right (32.4%) and far right (33%) readers. *El Confidencial* is centred in the middle (38.1%) and leans towards the right (38%), and *El Español* has a majority of right wing readers (29.6%). By age, the media outlet most attractive to those under 25 years of age is eldiario.es (66%). In contrast,

5.2 Degree of Information and Preferences

Table 5.4 Media commonly used to obtain information (%)

| | Average | Ideological self-positioning | | | | | Age | | | | | |
		Far left	Left	Centre	Right	Far right	16–24	25–34	35–44	45–54	55–64	65+
TVE	47.8	42.9	57.3	44.7	43.4	40.0	46.7	36.1	43.9	49.7	52.8	49.4
Antena 3	53.7	24.7	35.8	63.2	75.2	72.5	61.7	54.2	55.3	54.1	54.9	49.8
Tele 5	21.0	22.1	18.1	20.9	24.0	27.5	36.7	33.3	30.7	13.8	20.1	13.9
La Sexta	29.2	40.3	41.8	26.8	11.6	10.0	26.7	31.9	28.1	31.4	25.0	30.7
Radio Nacional	35.1	33.3	49.6	30.4	25.0	16.7	36.7	30.3	30.4	28.7	34.2	42.5
Cadena Ser	52.4	77.8	71.4	43.7	25.0	27.8	46.7	63.6	58.9	49.5	60.3	46.6
COPE	31.7	7.4	9.0	40.5	59.2	77.8	46.7	27.3	25.0	26.7	34.2	34.2
Onda Cero	31.7	20.4	19.5	35.4	50.0	44.4	13.3	27.3	26.8	37.6	28.8	35.6
El País	65.9	85.0	82.7	58.6	39.7	40.0	57.9	69.0	72.2	63.0	69.5	64.3
El Mundo	41.0	22.5	25.3	53.3	57.1	40.0	52.6	35.7	29.6	43.2	43.9	40.7
ABC	20.1	12.5	9.3	21.9	42.9	33.3	26.3	21.4	22.2	14.8	11.0	25.7
La Razón	11.4	5.0	8.0	14.2	12.7	26.7	18.4	7.1	13.0	12.3	7.3	12.1
El Diario.es	44.3	49.2	51.6	39.1	35.2	46.7	66.0	42.9	33.7	43.0	41.0	47.9
OK diario	21.5	12.7	12.0	28.2	32.4	33.3	24.0	14.3	19.6	17.5	20.5	31.1
El Confidencial	32.0	22.2	27.2	38.1	38.0	20.0	30.0	41.6	18.5	27.2	41.0	35.3
Público	28.8	61.9	34.2	21.8	8.5	13.3	20.0	23.4	43.5	20.2	33.7	29.4
El Español	17.8	1.6	10.3	25.2	29.6	20.0	20.0	14.3	18.5	24.6	15.7	13.4

OK Diario primarily attracts those over 65 years old, while *El Español* has a significant following among individuals aged 45 to 64. *El Confidencial* appeals notably to two age groups: 25 to 34 years (41.6%) and 55 to 64 years (41%), with less engagement from those in between.

Among all the media considered in the survey, *COPE* and *ABC* have a notably religious profile, with 58.5% of *COPE*'s followers and 40.0% of *ABC*'s followers identifying as practising Catholics.

5.3 Politicisation and Exposure

The politicisation of the media is considered one of the consequences of social polarisation and this perception of a lack of independence influences citizens' trust in the communication system in general and in certain information organisations specifically. To explore this aspect further, the survey asked participants to express their agreement with the statement: "The media should be politicised, defending an ideological stance" or, conversely, "The media should not be politicised, but rather apolitical and more neutral."

The results show overwhelming support (94.3%) for the view that the media should not be politicised, with only a small percentage supporting politicisation (4.7%). Paradoxically, this ideal is far from reality: 91.7% of respondents believe that the media are very or quite politicised, while only 3.3% feel they are little or not at all politicised (0.9%). The survey data indicate that the far right is most likely to view the media as highly politicised (64.9%), compared to 50.8% of the left, who generally regard it as "fairly" politicised.

These results are consistent with the 2022 Reuters Institute survey, which showed that Spain is one of the European countries with the lowest percentage of the population (13%) believing that the media are independent of political influence, compared to countries like Finland (50%) and the Netherlands (46%) (Newman et al. 2022).

The narrative that the media are partisan is based on a strong and exclusive preference among citizens for media that align with their views, a trend that intensifies over time (Newman et al. 2024). This trend contrasts with the majority of survey respondents (73.4%), who believe they choose to get information from media they consider "more balanced and objective", compared to 11.6% who admit to preferring those that "align more" with their thinking, a preference acknowledged by those identifying as far left (23.1%) or far right (21.1%). Furthermore, 4.7% of respondents seek news that offers perspectives different from their own, while one in ten claim to be indifferent.

The 2022 Digital News Report confirms the high level of polarisation in Spain, noting that—alongside Italy—it ranks second among the 46 countries included in the report, with a low percentage of the population convinced that news media are free from undue political influence (13%), just behind Greece (7%) (Newman et al. 2022). Spain ranks as the second country, following Poland (54%), with the highest

5.3 Politicisation and Exposure

Table 5.5 Ideological positioning of media outlets (scale 1 to 10)

				Ideological self-positioning					
	Average	M	F	Far left	Left	Centre	Right	Far right	Difference far left-far right
COPE	7.60	7.67	7.53	8.23	7.93	7.26	7.41	7.12	1.11
ABC	7.26	7.46	7.05	7.87	7.80	6.86	6.85	6.64	1.23
La Razón	7.01	7.16	6.85	7.83	7.64	6.57	6.43	6.16	1.67
El Mundo	6.67	6.75	6.58	7.39	7.12	6.24	6.35	6.26	1.13
Onda Cero	6.16	6.34	5.94	6.46	6.39	5.94	6.08	5.82	0.64
Antena 3	6.14	6.19	6.10	6.94	6.46	5.77	6.04	5.50	1.44
El Confidencial	5.75	5.83	5.66	6.48	5.75	5.58	5.45	6.20	0.28
Tele 5	5.54	5.59	5.49	6.54	6.22	5.27	4.62	4.00	2.54
El Diario.es	5.24	5.05	5.44	5.35	5.28	5.16	5.25	5.28	0.07
Radio Nacional	5.19	4.89	5.52	5.77	5.53	5.06	4.70	4.20	1.57
El País	4.82	4.70	4.95	5.67	5.04	4.79	4.21	3.59	2.08
Cadena Ser	4.80	4.59	5.04	5.27	5.03	4.82	4.23	3.64	1.63
TVE	4.79	4.58	5.00	5.37	5.30	4.71	3.87	3.85	1.52
La Sexta	4.33	4.23	4.43	5.16	4.66	4.19	3.73	3.15	2.01

proportion of its population believing the media to be highly polarised, at 49%. This perception contributes to a reduced sense of neutrality among citizens and a greater inclination to distrust the media (Kalogeropoulos et al. 2019).

The view of media politicisation among nine out of ten Spaniards is highlighted when respondents are asked to rate the political alignment of various media outlets on a scale from 1 (far left) to 10 (far right). Based on a sample of 14 prominent Spanish media outlets, including leading print, television, radio, and digital press, Spaniards generally position these outlets in the centre right, with scores ranging from 4.33 to 7.60 (Table 5.5).

The media perceived as most progressive include La Sexta, TVE, *Cadena Ser*, and *El País*, while *Radio Nacional*, Eldiario.es, *Tele 5*, and *El Confidencial* are positioned in the centre left (all with a score of 5). *Antena 3*, *Onda Cero*, and *El Mundo* are categorised as centre right (with 6 points), while *La Razón*, *ABC*, and *COPE* are seen as right wing (with scores exceeding 7).

These average positions vary widely based on respondents' ideological self-positioning, showing a clear tendency to rate media whose editorial line diverges from their own views as more extreme. Thus, the same media outlet can show a difference of over 2.5 points in perceived ideology, according to whether it is evaluated by someone from the far left or the far right. For instance, the ideological perception of *Tele 5* ranges from a centre-left position (5.54) to a centre-right position (6.54) among the far left, and left (4) among the far right.

Variations of up to two points also exist for *El País* and La Sexta, with their placement based on political leanings. While *El País* is perceived to be centre left by the far left (5.67), the far right places it on the left (3.59). La Sexta is considered closer to the far left when taking into account the views of the far right (3.15) and the centre left (5.16).

Generally, the consideration of ideological self-positioning shows variations of more than one point in six of the media considered, across both conservative and progressive groups. Alongside La Sexta—which the far right sees as the most left-leaning medium—the *COPE* network is rated as the most right-leaning (8.23), according to the left's assessment. The media showing the least distance between the ends of the ideological spectrum are the two digital outlets, eldiario.es and *El Confidencial*, along with *Onda Cero*.

When assessments are considered based on gender, women tend to rate media positioned as right or centre right slightly higher, as seen with *COPE, ABC, La Razón, El Mundo, Onda Cero*, and *Antena 3*. Conversely, they tend to view those identified as left or centre-left as more progressive. Among age groups, younger audiences lower the conservative assessment of *COPE, ABC*, and *La Razón*, while those over 25 (35 in the case of *ABC*) perceive these outlets as more conservative. Notably, younger individuals have a more conservative perception of the ideological positioning of the two media considered most progressive (*El País* and TVE).

Open Access This chapter is licensed under the terms of the Creative Commons Attribution 4.0 International License (http://creativecommons.org/licenses/by/4.0/), which permits use, sharing, adaptation, distribution and reproduction in any medium or format, as long as you give appropriate credit to the original author(s) and the source, provide a link to the Creative Commons license and indicate if changes were made.

The images or other third party material in this chapter are included in the chapter's Creative Commons license, unless indicated otherwise in a credit line to the material. If material is not included in the chapter's Creative Commons license and your intended use is not permitted by statutory regulation or exceeds the permitted use, you will need to obtain permission directly from the copyright holder.

Chapter 6
Quality of Information and Democracy

The origins of journalism and modern democracy are closely intertwined (McNair 2009). This concept is embedded in media theory (Christians 2009) and in the professional values of journalism (Deuze 2005). This is particularly seen in the role of a watchdog (Schudson 2008; Josephi 2013; Carson 2019), recognised as a means of scrutinising power and keeping citizens informed (Nethanel 2020).

This relationship is acknowledged in the constitutional protections afforded to journalistic activities in Western democracies. As Lacy and Rosenstiel note, this reflects a fundamental premise: "Individual decisions that aggregate to elect public officials are optimal when voters have access to large amounts of information and opinion" (2015, p. 9). From a normative perspective, journalism provides the necessary elements for citizens to contribute effectively to democracy. "It is a check against tyranny and abuse. More generally, journalism, by making information more transparent in society, is an essential ingredient for democratic self-government" (Lacy and Rosenstiel 2015, p. 9). Vehkoo adds, "journalism is the most accessible and, hopefully, most trustworthy source to obtain this knowledge" (2010, p. 5).

However, in recent decades, economic, political, and technological pressures (Witschge and Nygren 2009; Hanitzsch et al. 2019) have blurred the boundaries of journalistic activity, making it susceptible to conflicts with the ideals of providing truthful, public-interest-oriented information, adhering to the ethical principles of the profession, and fostering public debate (Schudson 2015). In such a context, the concept of quality journalism is essential as a cornerstone of an activity valued as a public good (Allern and Pollack 2019). Vehkoo emphasises: "A democracy can do without newspapers, but it cannot exist without quality journalism" (2010, p. 68).

According to McQuail, the main requirements for quality information are "truth", "relevance", "informativeness", and "impartiality" (McQuail 2005, p. 202). He believes that mass media should provide audiences with a wide range of relevant news and contextual information about world events. This information must be accurate and honest and as complete and faithful to reality as possible. Additionally,

McQuail highlights that information should be "reliable", in the sense that it should be verifiable and clearly separate facts from opinions. Lastly, it should be balanced and fair (unbiased), presenting alternative perspectives impartially and without sensationalism (McQuail 2005).

In line with this, in *The Elements of Journalism* (2001), Kovach and Rosenstiel outline nine tasks that journalism must fulfil to guarantee society the information it needs to be free and that citizens have a right to expect. Foremost among these are the journalist's obligation to truth and loyalty to citizens. They also stress the importance of verification, maintaining independence in the topics covered, serving as a counterbalance to power, and providing a forum for public criticism. Additionally, they highlight the commitment to citizens by ensuring that significant issues are presented in an engaging and relevant manner and that news is thorough and proportional. This ultimately means adhering to deontological rules in the practice of journalism.

The implications associated with journalistic quality have made this concept an essential element in debates about the state of journalism (Chen and Suen 2023) and a necessary measure when evaluating its impact on democratic quality (Lacy and Rosenstiel 2015). This is due to the unavoidable link between quality journalism and democracy (Casero-Ripollés 2016) and its indispensable role in democratic states (Allan 2009; Schudson 2008).

6.1 Definition and Identification

Academic explorations into the quality of journalism grapple with defining a complex, multi-dimensional concept tied to professional excellence (Gómez-Mompart et al. 2013; Meier 2019; Bachmann et al. 2023). Its intangible nature and several constraints complicate a clear approach to it within journalistic productions.

Primarily, its nature demands a holistic approach, integrating not only the conditions under which journalistic content is produced but also its presentation and reception (Gutiérrez-Coba 2006; Gómez-Mompart and Palau-Sampio 2013). This includes considering the needs and desires of citizens (McQuail 2012) and the context surrounding journalistic production (Vehkoo 2010).

The second challenge arises from varying approaches to the concept, which have highlighted different aspects since the introduction of the quality notion to the media field in the 1960s. Various traditions have focused on technical conditions, social responsibility, or the economic impacts of quality or its absence in journalistic enterprises. Sectoral perspectives, whether from journalists, editors, or audiences, and even from fields like politics or justice, apply differing criteria and assign them varying importance (Meier 2019). A third complexity is the blurred boundaries of journalistic activity in the digital environment (Malik and Shapiro 2016; Bachman et al. 2022).

Despite the difficulties in definition, various authors have emphasised the need to evaluate journalistic quality, establishing analysis patterns (Schulz 2000), either

6.1 Definition and Identification

through a formal measurement method or by identifying criteria. These approaches indirectly address the components of journalistic quality.

The paradigm of journalistic quality is associated with what is commonly termed the elite press, the large international benchmark media. One of the earliest approaches was by John Merrill, who, in 1968, identified five defining characteristics of quality press:

1. Independence, founded on financial stability, integrity, social concern, and the presentation and editing of content.
2. The value of opinion and interpretation, advocating a broad, global perspective free from sensationalism.
3. Emphasis on significant issues such as politics, international relations, economics, social welfare, and cultural, educational, and scientific matters.
4. A vocation to nurture, develop, and maintain an educated and competent audience.
5. The determination to influence international opinion leaders (Merrill 1968)

Among the most well-received proposals in the analysis of quality—especially in the Ibero-American sphere—is what is known as Journalistic Added Value (JAV), which considers elements of information selection (gatekeeping) and production (newsmaking) (Pellegrini and Mujica 2006). In the initial stage, indicators like news type, information origin, relevance (interpreted as proximity and consequence), and sources (considering the number, type, level, and contribution) are taken into account (Alessandri et al. 2001). The production stage of JAV considers three dimensions: style, content, and emphasis (Alessandri et al. 2001). Proposed at the start of the century, this model has seen several updates since (Pellegrini et al. 2011).

While the North American tradition has focused on journalistic quality linked to economic outcomes (Kovach and Rosenstiel 2001), recent years have seen a shift towards social contribution, with a focus on how reported facts benefit society (Ramírez de la Piscina et al. 2015). In line with this, the proposal by Lacy and Rosenstiel (2015), detailed in the document "Defining and Measuring Quality Journalism", merges professional variables with significant attention to the community it serves. For Lacy and Rosenstiel (2015), journalistic production quality is based on seven key elements:

- Quality of presentation, encompassing both formal aspects and community accessibility.
- Reliability, assessed through accuracy and credibility.
- Diversity, reflecting the range of sources, issues, themes, and ideas within the information and representative of the entire community.
- Depth and breadth of information, facilitating an understanding of issues and trends. In addition to examining important issues, this also involves making efforts to provide context through news and opinions: a variety of story presentation styles.
- Emphasis on the comprehensive nature of the published content, addressing significant community concerns.

- Focus on public affairs, emphasising information on major societal issues, government operations, education, and activities impacting community life quality.
- Geographic relevance, relating to events, issues, and trends significant to people within the primary coverage areas (Lacy and Rosenstiel 2015).

From a European perspective, Meier (2019) offers an approach to journalism quality combining classic professional values (independence, truth/factuality, relevance/context) with the activities performed and the final product from the audience's viewpoint. In this context, independence is articulated at both organisational and personal levels, reflecting the attitudes and opinions of professionals, evident through impartiality, balance, and a clear demarcation between facts and opinions.

Regarding truth and factualness, this value is associated with depth and impartiality, aimed at producing content that is diverse, transparent, interactive, and clear. Relevance or context is steered by professional principles that include the significance of topics, originality, novelty, editorial transparency, and the possibility of audience involvement in the editorial process or its translation into content. This is manifested in the content's ability to engage audiences, its utility, and its potential to offer solutions.

Spurk sets out ten conditions, which include: variety of sources, identification of issues beyond the official agenda, inquisitive questions, clarity in methodology, good formal structure, contextualisation of data, diversity of approaches, furthering the root causes of the issues and historical background, variety of viewpoints, and, if relevant, the response from the parties involved (Spurk 2019, pp. 28–29).

6.2 Perception of Journalistic Quality

Alongside the identification of journalistic quality indicators, their evaluation is a notably significant aspect. As Meier (2019) highlights, a common feature across various approaches is the recognised devaluation of journalistic standards. Despite the rise of digital media enhancing the intensity and assertiveness of critical evaluations (Bachmann et al. 2023), the discourse concerning the media's deficient quality is longstanding. Over a century ago, Lippmann (1922) identified a disconnect between public expectations and the media's delivery, which failed to provide the requisite quality to interpret a complex environment.

Beyond the studies that concentrate on the information product itself, delving deeper into the assessments of journalistic quality by analysing certain topics and through the perspectives of two crucial participants—professionals and audiences—would be of interest. Both perspectives are examined through empirical approaches, using evaluations from various surveys conducted in Spain.

6.2.1 The Journalists' Perspective

The assessment of quality by Spanish journalists paints a critical picture of their professional practice. This critique is not solely about quantity but more about the factors impacting their work. Comparing a 2013 survey involving over 300 journalists (Gómez-Mompart et al. 2015) with data from the 2020 professional survey by the Madrid Press Association (APM) reveals a bleak outlook: a majority of journalists believe that the quality of journalistic products is mediocre.

Research from a decade ago showed that 81% of journalists surveyed (N=363) felt that journalistic quality standards had declined over recent years, particularly due to the crisis in the sector (Gómez-Mompart et al. 2015). Journalists attribute this deterioration to the media's lack of economic and political independence, minimal business investment, and issues arising from technological shifts in a precarious job market. These problems persist and have intensified (see Chap. 7).

This exacerbation is apparent when journalists evaluate the quality of coverage on complex topics; nearly four out of five state that it is inadequate (APM 2020). Specifically, the 2020 *Annual Report of the Journalism Profession* by the Madrid Press Association (APM) reveals that 12% of journalists find it extremely deficient and 65% somewhat deficient. Against this, 1% consider it very good, while another 22% deem it acceptable (APM 2020, p. 76). Conducted during the COVID-19 pandemic, the survey queried whether the complexity of information had increased over the last two decades, a notion supported by 90% of respondents. Additionally, seven out of ten journalists stated that greater specialisation was needed (APM 2020, p. 76).

Another notable finding from the APM's series of reports on the journalistic profession points to poor quality as a primary reason for the public's dwindling trust in journalism. Analysis from 2014 to 2022 shows that the lack of rigour and quality consistently ranks among the top three concerns. In 2021, 45% cited it as the main issue after sensationalism (APM 2021), while by 2022, this figure had risen to 48%, positioning it as the second-most significant problem after the economic and political interests of editorial groups (APM 2022).

6.2.2 Audience Assessment

The Spanish audience's perception of journalistic quality presents a concerning picture. Nearly two-thirds of respondents believe that the content offered by the media is of low (41.1%) or very low quality (22%), compared to those who rate the quality as high (29.2%) or very high (2.5%) (Table 6.1). The most critical views align with higher educational levels and more extreme political positions. For instance, the assessments from individuals with a master's or doctoral degree (29.7%) are 15 points higher than those with a lower education level (14.3%) and those that are on political extremes—32.3% on the far left and 38.6% on the far right.

Table 6.1 Perception of media quality in Spain (%)

		Ideological self-positioning				
Assessment	Average	Far left	Left	Centre	Right	Far right
Very high	2.5	3.1	2.3	3.1	0.5	3.5
High	29.2	22.3	29.7	29.8	31.3	29.8
Low	41.1	40.0	46.3	37.1	46.7	26.3
Very low	22.0	32.3	16.9	22.3	18.7	38.6
DNK/DNR	5.2	2.3	4.8	7.7	2.7	1.8

Table 6.2 Perception of the evolution of media quality in Spain (%)

		Gender		Level of education					
Assessment	Average	M	F	Less than primary studies	Primary school studies	Intermediate studies	University graduate	Master and PhD	DNK/DNR
Has improved in recent years	19.8	16.3	23.0	28.6	27.1	24.8	15.0	11.5	12.5
Has got worse in recent years	49.9	56.1	44.2	42.9	37.4	41.7	60.3	58.1	37.5
Has remained the same, it was poor before and remains poor	22.9	21.1	24.6	–	26.2	24.4	18.8	27.0	37.5
Has remained the same, it was good before and remains good	7.4	6.6	8.2	28.6	9.3	9.0	5.9	3.4	12.5

When asked about the evolution of media quality over time, seven out of ten respondents indicated that it had worsened (49.9%) or remained at the same levels of mediocrity (22.9%) (Table 6.2). Conversely, only two out of ten respondents believe there has been a favourable evolution (19.8%) or that acceptable levels have been maintained (7.4%). Men (56.1%) tend to be more critical than women in assessing the decline in quality, as do individuals with university degrees (60.3%) or advanced degrees such as master's and doctorates (58.1%). By age group, those over 65 years old (58%) are most critical of the devaluation of quality, whereas respondents aged 45–64 are more inclined to believe that quality has improved (26.4%).

6.2 Perception of Journalistic Quality

Alongside the general perception of quality, the survey asked respondents about the causes of poor quality. Out of eight options related to formal aspects, external influences, and content presentation, politicisation (71.6%) emerged as the primary obstacle to quality, followed by sensationalism, noted by nearly half of the respondents (48.9%) (Table 6.3). Secondly, respondents pointed to issues concerning independence and transparency; economic interests of publishing and business groups (44.8%), and the blending of information and opinion (35.2%) were considered significant problems. Thirdly, deficiencies linked to a lack of rigour (27.1%), depth and explanation (20.7%), or journalist professionalism (16%) were noted. Hidden advertising was highlighted by 17% of respondents.

Ideological self-positioning reveals critical insights. The left (53.1%) and far left (47.7%) are more sensitive than average to the economic interests of publishing groups, while the far right highlights a lack of depth (28.1%) and journalist professionalism (26.3%). The impact of sensationalism is significantly lower among the far right (33.3%) compared to the left (57.9%) and far left (52.3%).

By age, the youngest respondents and those over 65 are least sensitive to politicisation (58.8%), but they rate the lack of depth above average (24.2%). Meanwhile, sensationalism is a prominent issue for the 35–44 age group (57.2%), and politicisation (81.6%) along with the economic interests of publishing groups are major concerns for the 55–64 age group (51.0%).

In addition to identifying the main quality problems, participants were asked which type of content was likely to generate these problems. The two areas that garnered the most consensus were related to power structures: political (79.4%) and economic (53.8%) (Table 6.4). Following these were topics affecting fundamental rights, such as healthcare (37.8%), education (22.7%), and gender equality (20.7%). In a third group were the environment (16.2%), social life (15.3%), science and technology (9.3%), sports (9.9%), and culture (8.6%).

Gender was an influential variable, with men (84.8%) more likely than women (74.4%) to view politics as problematic content, while women placed greater emphasis on healthcare concerns, surpassing men by ten points (42.7%). The level of concern correlated with each gender's interest in these topics. Age also influenced perceptions, with those over 65 finding the treatment of politics most problematic (92%), those over 55 focusing on healthcare (43.1%), and the youngest age group (under 25) expressing concern about environmental issues (22.4%). Political self-identification revealed that left-leaning individuals most clearly identified the potential problems in the coverage of politics (85.6%).

The survey indicates that public media do not enjoy particular prestige among citizens. In fact, respondents rated the quality provided by public (20.9%) and private (20%) media similarly, with 32.3% viewing them as equivalent (Table 6.5). Conversely, more than a quarter of those surveyed believe that neither offers quality content. When considering ideological perspectives, the positions on media ownership are revealing. The far left rates the quality of public media 16 percentage points higher than the average (36.9%), while the far right rates it ten points lower (10.5%). The situation is reversed for private media, with the far left rating them lower (7.7%)

Table 6.3 Aspects that most contribute to reducing quality (%)

Assessment	Average	Ideological self-positioning					Age					
		Far left	Left	Centre	Right	Far right	16–24	25–34	35–44	45–54	55–64	65+
The politicisation of the media themselves, and their connections with political parties	71.6	68.5	73.4	69.8	74.2	73.7	58.8	64.9	76.9	78.2	81.6	58.8
Opinion is intertwined with information	35.2	40.8	34.5	35.2	34.6	29.8	33.3	35.6	30.1	37.1	35.4	33.3
Lack of depth and clarity in explaining information	20.7	21.5	19.2	19.8	23.1	28.1	24.2	19.8	17.5	17.3	18.1	24.2
Sensationalism	48.9	52.3	57.9	44.4	45.6	33.3	50.3	45.0	57.2	51.3	48.6	50.3
Hidden advertising	17.1	13.8	16.7	19.0	15.4	17.5	24.8	20.3	15.3	17.8	11.1	24.8
The lack of professionalism among journalists	16.0	19.2	10.5	16.5	20.3	26.3	15.7	14.9	14.4	19.3	16.3	15.7
The economic interests of publishing groups and employers	44.8	47.7	53.1	39.6	42.9	36.8	43.8	40.1	46.3	45.2	51.0	43.8
The lack of rigour and the poor quality of information	27.1	26.2	29.4	25.6	26.9	28.1	28.8	26.7	24.9	24.4	29.2	28.8
Others	0.3	0.8	0.3	0.2	0.5	–	0.7	–	0.4	0.5	0.3	0.7
DNK	6.1	3.1	1.7	10.0	5.5	8.8	6.5	10.9	5.7	3.0	2.8	6.5

6.2 Perception of Journalistic Quality

Table 6.4 Content types most often associated with quality problems (%)

Assessment	Average	Ideological self-positioning					Age					
		Far left	Left	Centre	Right	Far right	16–24	25–34	35–44	45–54	55–64	65+
Politics	79.4	76.9	85.6	74.2	84.1	75.4	65.7	69.3	75.2	78.6	83.2	92.0
Economy	53.8	53.8	54.0	53.3	54.4	54.4	54.5	49.7	53.0	58.5	58.9	49.0
Sports	9.9	12.3	8.8	9.2	11.0	14.0	17.9	9.8	9.9	11.4	5.1	8.3
Environment	16.2	13.8	18.6	16.7	12.6	14.0	22.4	14.4	16.8	13.5	14.2	17.4
Health	37.8	36.2	33.6	41.5	36.8	40.4	26.9	34.0	36.1	35.8	43.1	44.1
Education	22.7	25.4	17.8	26.7	20.3	21.1	22.4	22.2	22.3	19.7	23.9	25.0
Science and technology	9.3	9.2	8.2	9.4	9.9	14.0	14.2	10.5	7.9	10.5	9.6	6.3
Culture	8.6	6.2	8.5	9.4	8.8	7.0	13.4	9.2	8.9	9.6	6.6	6.3
Social life, current affairs	15.3	18.5	15.0	15.2	13.7	15.8	17.2	22.2	12.4	14.4	17.3	12.2
Gender equality	20.7	23.8	22.9	16.9	25.8	15.8	22.4	28.8	22.3	23.1	16.2	15.6
Others	0.4	–	1.1	0.2	–	–	–	–	1.0	–	1.0	0.3
DNK/DNR	0.3	0.8	0.3	0.4	–	–	–	–	0.5	0.4	0.5	0.3

Table 6.5 Media that best guarantee quality, according to management and scope of coverage (%)

Modality	Average	Modality	Average
Public media	20.9	State media	18.5
Private media	20.0	Regional media	16.2
Both equally	32.3	Local media	16.3
None	26.8	All	14.6
		None	34.3

than the far right (35.1%), which shows greater support among right-leaning individuals (37.4%).

The field of dissemination reflects a distinctly divided opinion among those surveyed, with a third of the population indicating that none of the options guarantees quality. Regarding age, respondents under 34 years old tend to rate the quality of local media higher, whereas those over 55 place greater trust in state media. By autonomous community, Catalonia (9.7%) and the Basque Country (8.5%) rate the quality of state media ten points below the average, while the Basque Country (37.3%) and Catalonia (29.7%) emphasise the quality of regional media.

6.3 How Should Quality Improve?

In recent years, various international studies have focused on diagnosing the main quality issues in the media and offering solutions. In "Bias, Bullshit and Lies: Audience Perspectives on Low Trust in the Media", Newman and Fletcher (2017) explored the reasons underlying low trust in media across nine countries, including Spain. They concluded that for a significant part of the public, bias, misrepresentation, and hidden agendas carried more weight than public interest: "Simply put, a significant proportion of the public feels that powerful people are using the media to push their own political or economic interests, rather than represent ordinary readers or viewers" (2017, p. 5). These perceptions were particularly pronounced among younger people and those with lower incomes.

Newman and Fletcher (2017) suggested three key actions for the media to distinguish themselves from other online content: Firstly, the implementation of checking and verification processes and being transparent about information sources and corrections. Secondly, they emphasise the need to increase quality, investing in investigative and in-depth journalism, which stands out from general news. Thirdly, they highlight the need for a commitment to diversity to represent society as a whole, rather than focusing solely on elites. They also stressed the importance of combating bias and hidden agendas, advocating for greater transparency about these issues and funding sources. To regain public trust, they argued that media "will need to do more to rid news coverage of agendas and tired narratives, and bring a wider range of opinions into their coverage" (2017, p. 37).

6.3 How Should Quality Improve?

A variety of authors, all with a common focus on social commitment, have highlighted the need for a shift in the media's focus towards quality and content that is relevant to audiences. Katharine Viner—editor-in-chief of *The Guardian* since 2015—succinctly summarised the reasons for this change: "If journalists become distant from other people's lives, they miss the story, and people don't trust them" (Viner 2017).

This involves prioritising the contextualisation of information by offering analysis, depth, and perspective: "Journalism is something more than just an answer to 'who, what, where and when'. The more important questions to answer are 'why' and 'how' and 'what next'" (Vehkoo 2010, p. 75).

Costera Meijer and Bijleveld (2016) advocate for excellent journalism that impacts democracy, arguing that it must be consumed—read, watched, or heard—to be effective (p. 828). They propose the concept of *Valuable Journalism*, which explores the true reasons behind why people consume news, beyond assumptions by journalists or web metrics. This valuable journalism is based on four dimensions:

> First, *urgency* means that most people still want to keep up with important events and incidents close by. Urgency also refers to findability in connection to the platform as well as to the location of the event…
>
> Second, *public connection* stands out as the linking concept between respectfulness, a constructive approach, and supplying serious as well as light conversation topics. This might illustrate the importance of regional journalism for keeping up personal networks as well as people's identity as citizens.
>
> Our third suggestion is that the centrality of *understanding the region* within Valuable Journalism mirrors people's awareness of news as second-order reality; they know about others, and others know about them, in as far as and how they appear through news stories…
>
> Fourth, *audience responsiveness* is likely to mirror the growing assertiveness of the public. News media are expected to take into account and to listen carefully to the experiences of people of all walks of life, in interpersonal communication as well as in their stories (2016, p. 835).

In a subsequent study, Costera Meijer (2021) summarised her findings from a three-decade investigation into valuable journalism and identified three basic audience experiences: learning something new, gaining recognition, and enhancing mutual understanding. The first aspect stems from journalism that illuminates, broadens horizons, offers new perspectives, honours complexity, counterarguments, and is inspiring. The second aspect refers to concepts such as representation, listening, belonging, comfort, security, or affirmation. The third experience that valuable journalism offers includes empathy, empowerment, constructive meaning, hope, humour, and a sense of connection (2021, p. 236). The author highlights the challenge of aligning these three experiences with the six fundamental virtues of journalism in its relationship with the audience: "accuracy, sincerity, listening, hospitality, being a good friend and keeping a proper distance" (2021, p. 245).

One of the key demands from audiences, beyond the dissemination and interpretation of news, is for media to take greater responsibility by adopting the perspective of citizens and listening to their complaints and needs. The conclusions of the study conducted in the Netherlands by Van der Wurff and Schoenbach (2014) focused on more traditional demands, such as independence, the separation of information and

Table 6.6 Ways to improve quality (%)

Proposal	Average
With better contextualised information	33.1
With greater diversity of opinions	24.3
With information that deals with closer topics, that affect me more	11.3
With more variety of information	10.8
With non-politicised information	2.0
With more objectivity	1.2

advertising, the distinction between facts and opinions, diversity of viewpoints, and the correction of errors.

The expectations of the Spanish audience regarding how to improve the quality of information reflect the main considerations outlined above. For a third of respondents (Table 6.6), the primary demand is to improve the contextualisation of information as suggested by Vehkoo (2010). This requirement is particularly noted among those with master's or doctoral degrees (43.9%), those with left or far-left ideologies (38.1%), and individuals under 35 years of age.

A quarter of respondents emphasise that quality would increase with a greater diversity of opinions (24.3%), an option that becomes more significant after the age of 45. Additionally, focusing on more local issues is a priority for 11.3% of respondents, especially among younger individuals (14.2%) and those identifying as far-right (15.8%). One in ten respondents calls for more varied information (10.8%), with this diversity being particularly important to those identifying as right (14.3%) or far-right (19.3%), women (13.3%), and those under 25 years of age (14.9%). To a lesser extent, there are also calls for less politicised information (2%) and more objective presentation (1.2%).

In addition to identifying quality problems, the survey aimed to determine who is responsible for ensuring media quality. The majority of respondents believe this responsibility falls on journalists (63.1%) and media managers (61.1%) (Table 6.7). Those who focus responsibility most on journalists are individuals over 65 years of age (70.1%), with men (65.9%) more likely to do so than women (60.8%). Meanwhile, the 45–54 age group (66.4%) tends to attribute responsibility to media managers.

A notable finding is the increasing recognition of responsibility for media quality among society as a whole and the media audience (42.7%); a view more prevalent among men (46.9%), those over 65 (50.7%), and individuals with university (47.7%) or advanced degrees (47.3%). Ideological affiliation shows a greater inclination towards this responsibility among the far left (50.8%) and left (50.3%).

Respondents place the responsibility of citizens ahead of public authorities, who are responsible for legislating to ensure media quality (29.8%). This opinion is particularly strong among women (33.3%), those under 45, and individuals with master's or doctoral degrees (37.8%). In contrast, respondents from the far right are less supportive of this view (22.8%). The responsibility of external employers who financially support the media (22.1%) is highlighted above that of politicians in

6.3 How Should Quality Improve?

Table 6.7 Who should Be responsible for ensuring media quality? (%)

Assessment	Average	Gender		Age					
		M	F	16–24	25–34	35–44	45–54	55–64	65+
Managers or those responsible for the media	61.1	61.2	61.0	57.5	57.5	54.0	66.4	63.5	63.9
The journalists themselves who work in each media outlet	63.3	65.9	60.8	52.2	63.4	59.9	65.5	61.4	70.1
External employers who financially support the media	22.1	21.3	22.9	32.1	24.2	17.3	17.9	20.3	24.3
Politicians	14.1	14.0	14.2	17.9	15.0	15.3	11.8	12.7	13.9
Public authorities who do not legislate to control the media	29.8	26.1	33.3	32.8	32.7	32.2	27.9	28.9	27.4
Society as a whole, consumers of the media themselves	42.7	46.9	38.9	33.6	37.3	42.6	41.5	43.1	50.7
DNK	4.4	2.8	5.9	3.7	3.9	5.9	4.8	6.1	2.4
DNR	3.2	2.6	3.8	4.5	5.9	5.0	3.1	2.0	1.0

general (14.1%). Individuals under 25 are generally the most likely to attribute responsibility to both groups. It is notable that individuals who identify with right (28.0%) or far-right (31.6%) ideologies place much greater responsibility on economic powers compared to the left (19.5%) and far left (19.2%).

Despite the generally mediocre assessment of journalistic quality by the majority of those surveyed and the identification of journalists as the main people responsible for ensuring this quality, the survey responses reflect a moderate view when it comes to evaluating their work. When asked about their opinion of journalists and the work they do, the most common response was "neither positive nor negative" (35.1%), while one in three respondents rated it as "somewhat positive" (31.7%) and 13.9% as "somewhat negative". Although strong approval is modest (10.8%), it exceeds the percentage of respondents who view it as "very negative" by two points.

Open Access This chapter is licensed under the terms of the Creative Commons Attribution 4.0 International License (http://creativecommons.org/licenses/by/4.0/), which permits use, sharing, adaptation, distribution and reproduction in any medium or format, as long as you give appropriate credit to the original author(s) and the source, provide a link to the Creative Commons license and indicate if changes were made.

The images or other third party material in this chapter are included in the chapter's Creative Commons license, unless indicated otherwise in a credit line to the material. If material is not included in the chapter's Creative Commons license and your intended use is not permitted by statutory regulation or exceeds the permitted use, you will need to obtain permission directly from the copyright holder.

Chapter 7
Disruption in the Information Industry: Precariousness and Professional "Decapitalisation"

In recent years, the journalistic profession has been swept up in a whirlwind of changes and crises that have directly impacted not only the way activities are conducted but also the conditions of employment. The changes driven by the digitalisation of newsrooms have forced journalists to take on new responsibilities and tasks, resulting from the convergence of newsrooms (Salaverría-Aliaga et al. 2010) and the demands of multi-platform production (Doyle 2013). As several authors have noted, these processes have not been without problems, which have stemmed from the differing professional cultures and a lack of training to assume these new tasks (Killerbrew 2005; Salaverría-Aliaga et al. 2010).

Digitalisation has also presented new challenges in the search for viable business models to ensure the economic sustainability of the media. However, challenges in identifying sources of revenue have led to cost reductions, adversely affecting both the quantity and quality of employment. This crisis in the media model has been exacerbated by the effects of the financial crisis that began in 2008, which, coupled with a decline in advertising revenue, has destabilised media companies themselves. In addition to the closure of outlets and the restructuring of employment, there has also been the merger of television channels—such as Mediaset, resulting from the merger of Gestevisión Telecinco and Sogecuatro, and Atresmedia, formed by the merger of Grupo Antena 3 and Audiovisual Investment Manager—or the entry of investment funds and financial entities into the ownership of 20% of publicly traded media companies (Arranz 2019).

7.1 The Media's Multifaceted Crisis

Although the effects of the financial crisis were dramatic worldwide (Franklin 2014; Walker 2021), the Spanish journalistic industry has undergone a particularly devastating process. Advertising revenue for newspapers dropped from 1.894 billion euros in 2007, the year before the crisis, to 332 million euros in 2023 (InfoAdex 2008, 2024), representing a loss of more than 80%. Furthermore, the press has witnessed a collapse in its second source of income, news-stand sales. In February 2024, the total circulation of all daily newspapers published in Spain, nearly 80 titles, was under 876,637 copies per day, a 6.81% decrease from the same month in the previous year (Málaga Press Association 2024).

The figures show a dramatic decline, especially when considering that a decade earlier, daily sales exceeded 2.6 million copies (AEDE 2013). Compared to the results of 2007, only three newspapers, *El País* (435,000), *El Mundo* (336,286), and *ABC* (228,158), collectively reached a million copies in daily circulation (Arranz 2023). The print media sector is also facing rising costs due to the increase in paper prices, largely driven by conflicts such as Russia's invasion of Ukraine (AMI 2023).

In the television sector, advertising revenue has also declined, falling from 3.468 billion euros in 2007 to half that amount in 2023 (1.735 billion euros). Radio has also experienced a decline, although less severe, dropping from 678 to 461 million euros, a decrease of 32% (InfoAdex 2008, 2024). Simultaneously, the media have faced increasing competition from the Internet, with revenues in this sector rising from 482 million euros in 2007 to 2.810 billion euros, spanning search engines, websites, and social networks.

The crisis that unfolded at the end of the last decade in Spain led to the closure of 375 media outlets between 2008 and 2015, including newspapers, free media, magazines, television stations, radio stations, digital media, and news agencies (APM 2015). However, as the Madrid Press Association report cautions, these figures should be considered a minimum estimate, since "it is very difficult to track the fortunes of smaller media, especially those at a local level" (APM 2015, p. 92).

In addition to media closures and the shutdown of newsrooms, the effects of cost-saving measures imposed by companies—such as redundancies, employment regulation plans (EREs), early retirement, and budget cuts—have also been significant: 12,200 jobs have been shed since 2008. By sector, television (4459) and newspapers (2635) have been hit the hardest, followed by magazines (1589), media groups (1439), radio (880), free media (613), digital media (382), and agencies (203) (APM 2015, p. 92). Downsizing affects both those who lose their jobs and those who remain in the newsrooms (Ekdale et al. 2014, p. 383), as these cuts result in an additional workload for those who stay, a drastic change in employment conditions, and a decrease in income (Cohen et al. 2019; Sybert 2023).

These figures can be more precisely understood in the context of the devastating effects of the 2008 economic crisis, which particularly impacted the media sector. This crisis not only encompassed the direct effects of the financial downturn but also the collapse of advertising revenue, on which most media outlets were heavily or entirely dependent. Concurrently, the crisis took on a multifaceted nature by incorporating a third component: the transition the sector was undergoing from analogue to digital media. In essence, it was a triple crisis (López-García 2015; Calvo et al. 2024):

7.1 The Media's Multifaceted Crisis

– *Economic Crisis.* The Spanish economic model, which had produced high growth rates in the decade leading up to the crisis, was based on cheap credit following the introduction of the single European currency in 2002. This resulted in rapid expansion in the construction sector, with a significant increase in housing stock and prices. When the crisis hit, the real estate bubble in Spain burst, affecting all sectors related to construction and property transactions.

The Spanish media, like many other sectors fuelled by growth and investment optimism, had become financially exposed through large-scale investments. Expansion projects led the main Spanish communication groups to invest heavily in the acquisition of broadcasting rights (particularly for sports), new projects in the press, radio, television, and the Internet, and even in ambitious international expansion plans, especially in Latin America. The global economic crisis forced a rapid retreat from this strategy, leading to losses and even debt for media groups, many of which were compelled to sell their acquisitions at prices far below the original investment.

Furthermore, this slowdown also led to a lack of enthusiasm and even distrust towards the digital communications sector, similar to what happened after the bursting of the dotcom bubble in 2000, given the uncertainty about how investments in digital media would become profitable or even whether they would ever be recovered. On the other hand, by this point, most of the population was already online, and digital content had become a primary focus of consumption, making it unfeasible for media outlets to abandon this sector, despite the uncertainties it posed. So, the media remained online, albeit reluctantly, with minimal investment, precarious conditions, and staff cuts.

– *Advertising Crisis.* In addition to the inherent effects of the 2008 economic crisis, the media sector also had to contend with a significant decline in advertising investment, which was particularly severe in the real estate sector. It is important to note that on the eve of the crisis, the real estate sector accounted for more than 20% of total advertising investment in the media (López-García 2015), a figure that practically vanished for years as a result of the crisis. Other sectors of the economy that also invested in advertising significantly reduced their spending. It was not just that advertising disappeared or became less frequent, but the advertising that was contracted was done at much lower prices than those previously paid. As discussed earlier in this section, the collapse and subsequent reorientation of the advertising market had devastating effects on the media, as advertisers increasingly shifted their investment towards Google search results or social networks, to the detriment of traditional media.

– *Crisis in the Communications Sector.* As explored in depth in Chap. 2, the digitalisation process had profound effects on the communications sector. Naturally, this impact also triggered a painful and challenging process of industrial reconversion within news companies, as they transitioned from analogue to digital. The onset of the economic crisis within this context only compounded the difficulties, as the advent of the Internet was already causing discrepancies and differing opinions on how to handle the increasing speed of information and the changes this brought to the productive routines of newsrooms. This was particularly challenging for traditional print newspapers, which operated at a very different pace from radio and television (Calvo et al. 2024), with larger, more expensive structures and staff—although these were also more specialised and had better working conditions—compared to the emerging digital media that were beginning to replace them.

The shortcomings of the sector at all levels led to a significant shift in the business strategy of digital media over the past 5 years, with most outlets adopting various payment systems that resulted in the total or partial privatisation of information accessible to readers. This shift primarily demonstrated the advertising market's inability to cover the costs of the vast majority of media outlets.

7.2 Business Models and Their Alternatives

Since the emergence of the Internet, one of the most pressing challenges for media development has been finding ways to generate sufficient revenue from their content to achieve a return on investment or, at the very least, break even. As we have seen, this was an inevitable gamble for major media outlets, but it was often made without a strategic plan or a coherent long-term vision in an environment that was both rapidly changing and highly uncertain. The Internet became a space where the public expected to access all kinds of content for free, and initially, the media chose to satisfy that expectation. Over time, however, the internal dynamics of media companies, along with changes in other sectors linked to cultural industries (such as video games or the audiovisual sector), prompted media outlets to seek business models beyond monetising open content through advertising, as was typical for general television.

– *Advertising-Based Models*

Most "traditional" media outlets—those that existed before the advent of the Internet—relied on advertising for their revenue. Both radio and general television were almost entirely funded by advertising, while print newspapers (originally a classic paid media model) were partially financed through advertising, though they also charged readers a specific price. This model was attempted in new digital media, but it did not succeed: there were too many media outlets and too many content projects that, while not media, still competed for the advertising pie. Additionally, the advertising return in the digital landscape was much lower than in the analogue one, an apparent contradiction that persists to this day. Moreover, the presence on the Internet forces media outlets to make an extra effort to provide content in two increasingly divergent scenarios in terms of audience profiles, interests, and production rates.

7.2 Business Models and Their Alternatives

This has led media outlets, particularly in advertising-based models, to incorporate more advertisements and more aggressive, invasive campaigns for readers: "Large banners that occupy a significant portion of the header, which the user inevitably ends up clicking on even if they don't intend to; advertisements that suddenly jump to the foreground, annoying the reader, or even campaigns that occupy all the possible space around the media header. An invasive strategy that some outlets still maintain, and which has recently been intensified by the requirement to disable any ad blocker the user may have installed or to pay for browsing the site without accepting 'cookies'" (Calvo et al. 2024, p. 81). Additionally, the significant rise of branded content has further complicated the landscape, as it increasingly blends with non-sponsored content, leading to potential confusion for readers (Palau-Sampio and Iranzo-Cabrera 2024). Finally, it is important to highlight the media's activities within the business and institutional sectors, where they engage in partnerships with various industries, promoting sectoral activities in exchange for sponsorship.

– *Models Based on Paid Content*

As previously discussed, paid content models initially had a limited presence on the Internet, largely due to the open and free nature of content distribution that characterised the early days of the web. Moreover, in the Spanish context, the initial attempts to charge for journalistic content were unsuccessful. Both *El Mundo* and *El País* introduced subscription systems in the early twenty-first century (in 2002) but eventually abandoned them due to the low number of subscriptions, which was coupled with a noticeable decline in their influence within the digital public sphere. Since their content was not freely accessible, it received much less attention.

However, media outlets did not abandon the idea of monetising their content online, primarily because, as we have seen, the advertising market was insufficient to cover expenses. Additionally, there was a belief in the potential to "re-educate" the public. Just as the public had grown used to accessing journalistic content for free, they could be encouraged to pay for it—if the right approach was found. The key was to develop a payment system that would appeal to a sufficient number of readers or subscribers. Encouraging examples from other sectors, such as video games, the audiovisual industry, and the music industry through platforms like Spotify, suggested that a similar shift could occur in the consumption of current affairs content.

Thus, coinciding with the COVID-19 pandemic, many major Spanish media outlets began experimenting with various payment systems for content (Pérez et al. 2023), which largely followed models that had been tested in the past (Calvo et al. 2024):

– Partial or total paywall. In this model, access to part or all of the content requires a subscription (with options such as annual, quarterly, or monthly plans). Typically, only the front page and the first few lines of each article are visible without a subscription. This system is now the most prevalent among major Spanish media outlets online. Depending on the outlet, a subscription might be required for all content, or (more commonly in Spain) paid content—usually

unique to the outlet and requiring more effort to produce—is combined with freely available content from news agencies or branded content. This is the "Freemium" model, where content that does not require significant investment from the media and is not unique (because it comes from an external service, such as news agencies) is available for free and monetised through visits and advertising. Branded content, by its nature, is monetised as it is sponsored by companies and institutions that, since it is advertising content, want it to reach as wide an audience as possible.
- Metered paywall. This model, pioneered by the *Financial Times* in 2010 and later adopted by the *New York Times*, allows free access to a limited number of articles, after which the user must subscribe to continue reading (Calvo et al. 2024). In recent years, this model has fallen out of favour in Spain, after being applied in the past decade by reference media such as *El País* or *La Vanguardia*.
- Community of users and added services. In this model, the media outlet seeks to cultivate a sense of community and belonging among its most active users by offering them various benefits in exchange for their subscription. These benefits might include greater visibility in news comments, early access to the most important content, ad-free browsing, or access to certain exclusive content. The Spanish media outlet that has most successfully implemented this model is *eldiario.es*, which has over 70,000 members.
- Donations and crowdfunding. This approach, which involves seeking financial support from interested parties to fund various projects, has become very popular on the Internet. While some media outlets and freelance journalists have used it, it is more often employed to launch a media outlet or to fund a specific project (such as a report or documentary), rather than to ensure the long-term sustainability of a media outlet.

7.3 Changes in Structure and Values

The economic situation has impacted various aspects of the structure of the journalistic profession. One notable impact is the rise in self-employment, often in the form of so-called false self-employed workers, which entails fraudulent practices (Escalona 2019) and leads to precarious working conditions. In fact, changes in the ownership of certain media outlets have resulted in the replacement of staff editors with 'false freelancers' (FESP 2024). Additionally, there has been a 'decapitalisation' of journalism's watchdog role (Palau-Sampio and López-García 2022, p. 5), as most of the jobs created after the crisis have been absorbed by communication firms. The percentage of journalists employed by communications agencies and the communications departments of companies, public bodies, and institutions rose from 41% in 2012 to 47% in 2014 (Corral 2015).

This shift means that the relative recovery of employment has not contributed to strengthening human resources for investigative and informational tasks—crucial for the media's role as a watchdog—but has instead reinforced public relations and their influence on editorial content. In summary, under-resourced newsrooms with increased workloads have increasingly relied on press releases and statements to meet production demands, as highlighted by various studies (Macnamara 2016; Sallot and Johnson 2006).

The global precariousness and 'deprofessionalisation' experienced by journalism (Witschge and Nygren 2009) not only impacts professional careers (Deuze and Witschge 2018; Örnebring and Möller 2018), but also undermines the core of professional values. Commercial (Goyanes and Rodríguez-Castro 2019), political, and business pressures on professionals ultimately affect their work. Reports from the Madrid Press Association indicate that three out of four Spanish journalists have faced pressure in their professional duties on one or more occasions (APM 2022).

In parallel, working conditions have driven a growing hybridisation of journalistic activity, which blurs its essence (Witschge and Nygren 2009). The rise of branded content, presented as a lifeline to recover advertising revenue (Ferrer-Conill 2016), distorts professional values by presenting content that appears informative but actually serves the interests of the brands that finance it (Palau-Sampio and Iranzo-Cabrera 2024). This mimicry (Hardy 2017) transfers not only the characteristic style of the medium to advertisers but also editorial control over the content it includes (Palau-Sampio 2021b).

7.4 Precarious Work and Its Manifestations

Although "the journalism labour market has long been based on an oversupply of workers eager to enter the profession" (Örnebring 2018, p. 109), leading to various forms of unpaid work in the sector (Bakker 2012) or casual work in the newspaper industry (Cohen 2016), it is only recently that scholars have begun to focus on the instability of journalism (Örnebring 2018), resulting from "an intersection of economic, technological, and cultural factors that have contributed to the increasing job instability of professionals and the deterioration of their working conditions" (Besbris and Petre 2020, p. 1).

The communications sector in Spain has become increasingly precarious due to the multiple disruptions experienced by the journalistic industry (Curran 2010) and the implementation of neoliberal models as a survival strategy by journalistic companies (Moisander et al. 2018).

The International Labour Organization (ILO) introduced the concept of precariousness in 1974. However, although the term 'precarious work' is beginning to be used internationally, its definition remains ambiguous. In fact, the perception and experience of precariousness can vary between individuals and may relate to both the direct employment situation within a company and one's position in society at large (ILO 2012). The concept of precariousness is defined by several factors, including job-stability uncertainty, the number of potential employers, and the type of employment relationship, which can sometimes be concealed (ILO 2012, p. 27). Additionally, characteristics such as inadequate financial remuneration, limited opportunities for career and skills progression, lack of job security, and integration into the social security system further compound precariousness. Other issues include restricted access to social protection and employment benefits, as well as legal and practical obstacles to joining a union and engaging in collective bargaining (Keller and Seifert 2013; Norbäck and Styhre 2021).

7.5 Experiences in the Spanish Context

The results of two focus groups—one with junior journalists (under 35 years old) and one with senior journalists (over 40 years old)—have shed light on the extent of job insecurity among professionals in the sector in Spain. The relevance of this concern is underscored by the fact that, among the terms used in both sessions to describe the current state of journalism, "precarious" and "precariousness" were the only ones repeated in response to the moderator's question: "If we talk about journalism today, what is its current state? What words can we use to describe it?"

These terms were accompanied by others that reinforced this focus, either in diagnosing the situation or identifying contributing factors, such as "crisis", "versatility", and "immediacy". When it came to analysing the circumstances, the two sessions confirmed that the various factors associated with the definition of precariousness are clearly present in the working environment of journalism.

Job stability, or the lack thereof, is one of the primary concerns linked to job insecurity, particularly for younger journalists. A participant in the junior journalists' panel, aged 27, noted that since finishing her degree, she has been intermittently linked to the same media outlet for 5 years—"I have been coming and going"—and moving through different sections: "And now I'm back working in [section name], and still, I've never had a permanent contract in my life. I come and go, but I'm still there" (F1J). [The first initial corresponds to gender (F: female; M: male); the number corresponds to the participant's identifier in the group; the final letter indicates participation in the senior (S) or junior (J) group]. In other cases, as pointed out by a 28-year-old journalist, the contract does not arrive until after a long series of steps, including curricular internships: "In the summer of my third to fourth year at university, I did an internship at [media outlet], on the politics desk, and when the internship ended, they gave me a precarious contract, then a training contract, then a temporary contract, and finally they hired me" (M5J).

One problem highlighted is the inability of the industry to absorb the demand for employment from young journalists. A senior journalist in a leadership position at a media outlet pointed out that "the selection process is extremely competitive": "I've seen it in young people who have come up to me and asked me. These are individuals who have done the work, who have joined the media, and are now frustrated because they have a real calling but hit a wall—they can't get stable contracts, they can't secure more or less acceptable salary levels, they can't build a life. It wasn't like this 20 or 25 years ago" (M2S).

7.5 Experiences in the Spanish Context

One of the changes noted by the two focus groups is that the reduced opportunities to obtain a contract have also altered the new generations' tolerance for waiting indefinitely for one, whereas a few years ago this could have been justified: "There's no longer the prospect of 'I'll work for free because they'll give me a contract soon'" (M3S). One junior participant noted the rapid evolution: "From the generation in which I entered as an intern, when there were hundreds of thousands of us, to now having to ask people to please stay. People have already seen that this is how it is, and it's much less attractive... before there were always enough interns for a training contract (...) 'A colleague left six months ago and his replacement was only hired two weeks ago, they were behind from the start...'" (M5J).

The limited opportunities also lead to low loyalty to companies, as one junior journalist observes: "Hiring a journalist is so easy because we are paid so poorly and have little incentive to stay, aside from the fact that there aren't many better-paying opportunities elsewhere. You're doing a lot of hours and carry significant responsibility with the people you interact with daily... and all for a salary that makes you think: 'It's just not worth it'" (M4J).

Precarious employment conditions often include inadequate financial compensation, especially when working hours and availability demands exceed those established in the contract. "Salaries are very low compared to other sectors. Even for those who have been working in this sector for years" (F5S). In this context, the need for companies to cut costs also impacts senior journalists and their prospects for advancement: "Media companies, like any business, need to reduce salary costs, so they let go of those who are more expensive. It's becoming increasingly difficult to climb the corporate ladder" (M3S).

In some instances, the salary a journalist earns becomes a barrier to exploring more fulfilling professional options: "Right now, I have the best salary I've ever had. But I know that if I change environments, my salary would automatically drop" (M2S). This is compounded by the overall decline in wages in the sector relative to the demands: "I've come back to journalism after eight years, and the industry has changed in ways I didn't realise while I was away. Salaries have dropped to half of what they were eight years ago. Are we the only profession where wages decrease? Well yes, it's very likely. And the work I did eight years ago is very different from what my colleagues are doing now—significantly so" (M3S).

The low salaries are precisely what drive some journalists to leave the media and move into institutional communication roles. "I just made that switch. I'm earning double what I was. A little more than double what I was earning at a certain media outlet (...) For someone in their twenties, that salary is quite good. But when you're nearing 30 and see your friends who started alongside you doing better, and you're stuck in the same place..." (M5J).

Comparing their situation with other sectors or with people they know highlights the limitations of their salary compared to their professional responsibilities. "On the political desk, we work with politicians—people who earn three times as much as we do and with whom we interact normally, obviously. So, there comes a point where you think: 'I'm here, interacting with this person every day, and they're earning three times as much as I do, and honestly, they don't do much more than I do'. And in the end, you just think: 'I'm dealing with a lot of stress for what I earn'" (M4J).

Working hours become a critical factor, both in terms of salary and work-life balance. "There are people around you with more regular hours or higher, more stable salaries… So you start to think: 'Is this really worth it?'" (M3J). In fact, balancing work with personal life becomes a significant challenge: "I'd love my job if I didn't have another life. If I had no life outside of writing, I'd enjoy it very much. The problem is when you want a life outside of work, but it disrupts your plans—you arrive late to dinners, or have to cancel them, or you're at home trying to watch a film, and then you get a call, and you have to deal with it" (M1J).

Both experienced and younger journalists are committed to improving schedule management to better balance work and personal life, ensuring necessary rest and disconnection: "I think the schedules could be more condensed… Obviously, some things happen occasionally, and maybe a couple of people need to be available in the afternoon because things happen. But I think that by five o'clock, we could be done with work. In my case, I had to request a reduction in my working hours because I couldn't balance my work and family life. I work five and a half hours, but it feels like working eight—you cram everything into those five and a half hours… If we spend the whole day working and get home at nine at night, you have no personal life, no social life, and that takes a toll in the end" (F1S). The analysis suggests that companies exploit the vocational nature of the profession to extract maximum effort from their workers: "The media take advantage of the fact that journalism is a very vocational profession to keep exploiting you because they know you'll stay out of conviction, but they don't offer you what you truly deserve in terms of working conditions" (F3J).

When assessing the causes of the current situation in the sector, journalists point to structural issues, such as the lack of a viable business model, as being responsible for the lack of resources: "I agree that the business model needs to be more clearly defined so that it's sustainable in every sense—that is, it provides information and is profitable, but also improves workers' conditions, allows for honest work, and enables the creation of more thoughtful, in-depth reports or articles that provide more comprehensive information, and ultimately, truly inform society" (F1J). The absence of a viable business model for journalism has two clear consequences.

Firstly, it fosters a dependency that undermines the autonomy of the media: "That's the problem with journalism that relies on subsidies. For example, we [referring to the type of media] get 80 or 90% of our income from subsidies provided by the Generalitat [the Valencian regional council], provincial councils, city councils… and it doesn't matter which party is in power… in the end, they're the ones who have to give us the money to survive" (F1S).

When the moderator of the senior journalists' group asked: "Is there any censorship by media groups?" One of the participants replied without hesitation: "Yes, of course" (F3S). When asked whether there was any pressure, another journalist added: "Of course, there are interests. These are companies that have clear interests" (F5S). One participant elaborated on the censorship situations occurring in a

7.5 Experiences in the Spanish Context

specific media company: "There are instances of censorship. For example, 'this topic cannot be discussed,' 'this cannot be published'. 'X called me and said this. So I am going to change that headline'". This is happening... It's harmful and serious because it is degrading the profession; it's demoralising professionals, discouraging them—those who no longer want anything to do with it, due to job insecurity... This profession has a component of vanity... "People read my work". "That thing you told us". "I read something you wrote". We live off that deep down, and it's not something money can buy. It's paid for by your ability to publish, to have influence... But if they don't pay you, and they're paying you less and less, and you don't have the ability to attract attention because you don't want to stir things up, and because your media company doesn't want to stir things up, then it's over. The profession loses its incentives" (M2S).

Secondly, the lack of human resources in newsrooms leads to a dependence on press offices and agencies, as well as insufficient time to produce quality journalism. One of the participants, who works in a communications agency, describes this situation: "From outside the media, I know people who are incredibly capable, but their working conditions prevent them from doing their job well or reporting thoroughly. Sometimes I contact them, and they say, 'Mate, just give it to me ready-made so I can publish it, because I just don't have the time, I can't.' And that shouldn't be your job. Your job is to provide them with the information and details, but they should be the ones to work on the story, because in the end, that's what drives you as a journalist. 'Okay, I'll provide you with the information from an external source. I'm going to try to be as honest and thorough as possible. You're going to trust me, you're going to publish it because you're the one in the middle, but it shouldn't work like that'" (F3J). Another journalist admitted: "We all end up with the same, because when it's well done, it gets copied and pasted" (M5J).

According to journalists, task overload is one of the main barriers to quality journalism: "For me, offering more complete information also means covering fewer topics but with better quality, which seems like a utopia, but only slightly. That way, at least something could change. You can't just churn out four pieces in one day. It's impossible—they'll end up being rubbish, and in the end, you reduce the information to what a guy making a video gives you, and that's it. And that's a shame. It sucks because we're supposed to have the skills to prevent that. So, less journalism, but of higher quality. I have always thought that would be good" (M3J).

When considering future prospects, both younger and more experienced journalists paint a bleak picture. "We all enjoy what we do, but by the time you reach 50, you're burnt out... I remember when I joined [media outlet] a year and a half ago, one of the first meals I had while networking with colleagues... the age of the people working there was 45 and older, or between 35 and 45.... And I asked them: 'If you were to study a degree now, would you study journalism?' And everyone said no, except [one colleague]. They started suggesting all sorts of crazy jobs: 'I'd apply to be a librarian', things like that. None of them would have chosen journalism again. And I thought: 'What are you all doing here?'" (M3J).

Those with more experience find it difficult to imagine continuing in journalism under the current conditions until they retire. "I'd like to retire doing something related to journalism that still sparks my interest. But realistically, I can't see myself doing another 20 years in the same place, earning the same, and being able to live in Valencia… I mean, it's really hard to picture, one participant admitted" (F2S).

"I'd like to retire doing what I do now, but honestly, it feels like a pipe dream… Continuing in a profession that eventually pushes you out—you don't choose to leave—is very challenging. It won't be my choice" (F4S). The same participant later added: "I don't know if there is another profession where most people feel they need to have a plan B. I've been thinking about a plan B for ten years now" (F4S).

In seeking alternatives, some journalists have taken steps to open up new career paths, despite their love for their current work: "Last year, I completed a teaching master's degree as another career option because when my reduced work/life balance option ends, I'm not going to be available all the hours they want me to work… My personal life is very important to me. So if my job doesn't allow me to balance my personal life with work satisfactorily, then I'll have to find a career that will" (F1S).

While some have explored alternative options, they also recognise the risks involved. "This is a profession that loses its appeal when it becomes routine… you work long hours, give it a lot of mental energy, and you're on 24/7. It's hard to disconnect from it. When it becomes routine, you start to lose the idealism, and that often leads to thoughts like, 'I'd like to change my role or what I do within the same profession or something.' You can't do that right now in Valencia… especially not people our age. And it's a bit overwhelming… We're all kind of too dependant, you know? Too much: 'Damn, I'm not moving, just in case.' First because we have responsibilities, we have children etc." (M2S).

Open Access This chapter is licensed under the terms of the Creative Commons Attribution 4.0 International License (http://creativecommons.org/licenses/by/4.0/), which permits use, sharing, adaptation, distribution and reproduction in any medium or format, as long as you give appropriate credit to the original author(s) and the source, provide a link to the Creative Commons license and indicate if changes were made.

The images or other third party material in this chapter are included in the chapter's Creative Commons license, unless indicated otherwise in a credit line to the material. If material is not included in the chapter's Creative Commons license and your intended use is not permitted by statutory regulation or exceeds the permitted use, you will need to obtain permission directly from the copyright holder.

Chapter 8
Conclusions

This work aimed to synthesise the findings of a research project coordinated by its two authors. The research is the culmination of decades of academic reflection, conducted through teaching and successive studies on the transformations occurring in the field of communication. A central focus has been on the challenges the media ecosystem faces in adapting to these transformations, which have also affected the public, a matter we have also sought to analyse.

The book presents empirical results drawn from surveys and focus groups, all integrated into the theoretical reflections that we have tried to express throughout these pages. For a variety of reasons, stemming both from the empirical research base and our knowledge of the context, the analysis is primarily focused on Spain, which we believe represents the problems and challenges that Western democracies face. Moreover, we think that this analysis can, in certain contexts, be extrapolated to other regimes and sociocultural settings.

In this respect, the book provides a comprehensive overview built on four key axes:

- The digitalisation process and its influence on redefining the public sphere
- The socio-political context, focusing on three major dimensions that most strongly influence the current ecosystem: polarisation, populism, and misinformation
- Audience consumption habits and their assessment of journalistic products and quality
- The industry and the profession of journalism

Regarding the digitalisation process, the book delves into its unique characteristics: the profound changes it has brought about in the media sector and in the communication ecosystem as a whole. Digitalisation has enabled access to the creation and the dissemination of content by all kinds of actors who, in the previous scenario, played a primarily passive role, relegated to the position of mere spectators in a world where media mediation was widespread and inevitable.

The digitalisation process has impacted this mediation—this central role of the media—from many different perspectives. However, we can summarise its profound effects by noting that it affects the communication process as a whole, fundamentally altering the nature of the communication between sender and receiver, as well as the message itself. Consequently, it also changes the role of the audience, who now adopt diverse roles, acquiring new identities and facets in the digital communication landscape. It also modifies the relationship between social actors and the media. These actors can now create and disseminate their own content via communication systems that are not strictly part of the traditional media. However, the success of their messages often still depends on media coverage, which is more likely if these social actors have significant public visibility due to their field of activity.

The conclusion of this first area of interest in our research, which is fundamentally reflective and based on theoretical references, is that media outlets, despite other circumstances, see their role weakened in the digitalised landscape compared to the pre-existing one. This is evident in the reconfiguration of the public sphere, which is evolving from a structure almost entirely controlled by and dependent on the media to a constantly changing post-media public sphere.

Regarding the socio-political context, the book maps this by exploring the three dimensions that most influence the current ecosystem: polarisation, populism, and disinformation.

The survey revealed a fertile ground for the support of populist arguments: populist statements about political, economic, and media power were agreed upon by more than three-quarters of the respondents. However, proximity may play an important role, as when asked about international institutions, the level of support for populist arguments was lower.

The survey also showed significant polarisation around key issues such as migration, housing occupation, gender equality, climate change, and the erosion of traditional Spanish values. In general, the results present a scenario of agreement/disagreement that reveals a division of 40–60% of the population. There is, however, a broader consensus on certain issues: more than eight out of ten Spaniards support the recognition of sexual identity as an advancement in human rights, and more than seven out of ten support the measures taken in response to the pandemic, viewing them as necessary actions for an exceptional health situation.

Three-quarters of respondents indicated that disinformation is a significant issue, consistent with findings from other studies. The rise of social media and the Internet has been widely blamed for contributing to the problem of disinformation. Social networks and websites with false content or pseudo-media are seen as the primary sources of disinformation, ahead of political parties, economic powers, and the government. However, there are differences associated with gender, ideology, and age, which provide interesting nuances and merit further investigation in future research.

The perception of disinformation as a problem aligns with widespread support for public authorities to intervene in combating it. There is support for less radical measures, such as financial penalties or media literacy initiatives, as opposed to more extreme measures like shutting down broadcasts or banning publications.

8 Conclusions

In terms of audience behaviour, responses regarding actions taken when encountering potentially false content and precautions before sharing information suggest a seemingly responsible attitude on social media. However, some behaviours would require further exploration using qualitative analysis techniques, particularly to understand why people are more inclined to share or comment on content they agree with versus content they dislike.

Regarding audiences: The analysis covered both perceptions of the level of information and the type of content. There is a generally positive perception of the level of information, despite the fact that most individuals obtain their information through social media platforms. News avoidance is linked to an overload of advertising and lengthy content. This contrasts with the audience's view that poor contextualisation of information is a significant issue associated with journalistic quality. Similarly, there is a contrast between the audience's perception that local news and high-priority topics (hard news: healthcare, the economy, and politics) are the main areas of interest to the public, despite the actual viewing figures of such topics in digital editions.

The findings from comparing the media used for general information, the media used for obtaining more in-depth knowledge on specific news, and the media perceived to offer higher quality or more verified information underscore the need for qualitative studies that will help uncover the core aspects of information consumption. In fact, television remains the most widely used medium for obtaining information, and it is also regarded as the source providing the highest-quality or most trustworthy information. Additionally, it is crucial to examine the role of search engines as a tool for in-depth information gathering.

Media consumption shows a clear correlation between the media people use and their ideological self-positioning. There is widespread support for the belief that the media should not be politicised, while only a small minority favours political bias. Paradoxically, this ideal is far from reality: 91.7% of respondents believe that the media are very or quite politicised, while only 3.3% feel they are little or not at all politicised (0.9%). This discrepancy is further emphasised by the fact that media outlets tend to cater to audiences who seek out perspectives they already agree with, leading to a feedback loop between media and the public. This trend contrasts with the majority of respondents' belief that they opt for outlets they perceive as "more balanced and objective", while a smaller group admits to favouring those that align more closely with their personal viewpoints.

This pattern is reinforced by the tendency to view media with opposing editorial stances as more extreme. Thus, the same media outlet can show a difference of over 2.5 points in perceived ideology, depending on whether it is evaluated by someone from the far left or the far right.

As for the perceived quality of media content, the public generally believes that it is poor and has declined in recent years. Political content is seen as the most problematic, followed by economics and healthcare—ironically, the three areas that attract the most public attention. Alongside a desire for better contextualisation of information, there is a call for greater diversity of opinions. Indeed, the politicisation of the media and their links to political parties are seen as the biggest contributors to declining quality, along with sensationalism and the commercial interests of publishing groups and owners. Despite this, as we have seen, much of the public continues to engage with ideologically aligned media.

Citizens are quite clear when it comes to placing significant responsibility for the quality of information on media managers and journalists. The final focus of the analysis, which examines the media industry and journalism as a profession, highlights these actors to offer both a diagnosis and potential solutions to the issues identified by the public. One of the key conclusions from this empirical research is the complex situation facing the journalistic profession. Amid a crisis of trust in the media, its main advocates—the journalists—are grappling with the various aspects of job insecurity. These issues manifest at multiple levels:

- Mental health challenges, including stress, workload pressures, and difficulties balancing work and personal life.
- Insufficient time to produce high-quality journalism, conduct investigations, and thoroughly explore topics, as well as a reliance on communications departments when they are unable to fully develop stories.
- The challenges faced by younger journalists in securing quality jobs with fair pay. In some instances, they are caught in a cycle of precarious contracts. A generational sense that their work is of poorer quality and offers fewer opportunities for advancement compared to their peers in other professions.
- Pressures on journalistic independence and autonomy, stemming from economic difficulties and dependence on advertising revenue.
- Senior journalists with long-standing permanent contracts express doubts about whether they will be able to retire under the same employment conditions and are reluctant to switch outlets, aware that they would likely struggle to find similar terms.
- Senior journalists also express sympathy for the precarious conditions facing the younger generation.

The findings also highlight the importance of conducting more qualitative research into audience behaviours, particularly regarding their needs and preferences, considering key factors such as age and ideological self-positioning. Furthermore, it is vital to better understand public perceptions of journalistic quality and how people identify disinformation, particularly their awareness of its impact on democratic society. It is equally important to explore how the public confronts information that challenges their ideological viewpoints.

8 Conclusions

Open Access This chapter is licensed under the terms of the Creative Commons Attribution 4.0 International License (http://creativecommons.org/licenses/by/4.0/), which permits use, sharing, adaptation, distribution and reproduction in any medium or format, as long as you give appropriate credit to the original author(s) and the source, provide a link to the Creative Commons license and indicate if changes were made.

The images or other third party material in this chapter are included in the chapter's Creative Commons license, unless indicated otherwise in a credit line to the material. If material is not included in the chapter's Creative Commons license and your intended use is not permitted by statutory regulation or exceeds the permitted use, you will need to obtain permission directly from the copyright holder.

References

Abramowitz, Alan I., and Steven Webster. "The Rise of Negative Partisanship and the Nationalization of US Elections in the 21st Century." Electoral Studies 41 (2016): 12–22.
AEDE, Asociación Española de Editores de Diarios. Libro Blanco de la Prensa Diaria 2014. Madrid: AEDE, 2013.
AIMC. 2023. https://reporting.aimc.es/index.html#/main/radio
Alessandri, Francisca, Juan Carlos Edwards, Silvia Pellegrini, Sebastián Puente, Eduardo Rozas, Gonzalo Saavedra, and William Porath. "VAP: Un Sistema Métrico de la Calidad Periodística." Cuadernos.Info 14 (2001): 112–120. https://doi.org/10.7764/cdi.14.187
Aleixandre-Benavent, Rafael, Lourdes Castelló-Cogollos, and Juan C. Valderrama-Zurián. "Información y Comunicación Durante los Primeros Meses de Covid-19: Infodemia, Desinformación y Papel de los Profesionales de la Información." Profesional de la información 29, no. 4 (2020).
Allan, Stuart, ed. The Routledge Companion to News and Journalism. Oxon: Routledge, 2009.
Allern, Sigurd, and Ester Pollack. "Journalism as a Public Good: A Scandinavian Perspective." Journalism 20, no. 11 (2019): 1423–1439. https://doi.org/10.1177/1464884917730945.
AMI, Asociación de Medios de Información. "El Elevado Precio del Papel Prensa y su Carestía, Nuevo Desafío para los Medios de Información." 2023. https://www.ami.info/el-elevado-precio-del-papel-prensa-y-su-carestia-nuevo-desafio-para-los-medios-de-informacion.html.
APM, Asociación de la Prensa de Madrid. Informe Anual de la Profesión Periodística 2015. 2015. https://www.apmadrid.es/wp-content/uploads/2016/11/INFORME-PROFESION-APM-2015_baja_7M.pdf.
APM, Asociación de la Prensa de Madrid. Informe Anual de la Profesión Periodística 2020. 2020. https://www.apmadrid.es/wp-content/uploads/2021/11/Informe-Anual-profesion-periodistica-APM-2020-web.pdf.
APM, Asociación de la Prensa de Madrid. Informe Anual de la Profesión Periodística 2021. 2021. https://www.apmadrid.es/wp-content/uploads/2022/10/Informe-anual-Profesion-Periodistica-2021_web_lite.pdf.
APM, Asociación de la Prensa de Madrid. Informe Anual de la Profesión Periodística 2022. 2022. https://www.apmadrid.es/wp-content/uploads/2023/11/Informe-Anual-22_web_lite.pdf.
Arendt, Hannah. La Condición Humana. Barcelona: Paidós, [1958] 1993.
Asociación de la Prensa de Málaga. "El Informe de KPMG para la Asociación de Medios de Información Revela una Caída del 6,81% en la Distribución Respecto a 2023." 2024. https://aprensamalaga.com/sala-de-prensa/noticias/la-difusion-en-prensa-en-papel-no-llega-al-millon-de-ejemplares-diarios-20240416115692.html.

Arranz, Rodrigo. "Fondos de Inversión y Bancos ya Controlan el 20% de los Medios Cotizados." El Independiente, 18 September 2019. https://www.elindependiente.com/series-y-television/comunicacion/2019/09/18/fondos-de-inversion-y-bancos-ya-controlan-el-20-de-los-medios-cotizados/

Arranz, Rodrigo. "Las Cenizas de la Prensa en 2023: Tan Sólo 'El País' Vende Más de 50,000 Ejemplares Diarios." Vozpopuli, 11 November 2023. https://www.vozpopuli.com/medios/cenizas-prensa-2023-el-pais-ejemplares.html.

Bakker, Piet. "Aggregation, Content Farms and Huffinization: The Rise of Low-Pay and No-Pay Journalism." Journalism Practice 6, no. 5–6 (2012): 627–637. https://doi.org/10.1080/1751278 6.2012.667266.

Barber, Michael, and Nolan McCarty. "Causes and Consequences of Polarization." In Solutions to Political Polarization in America, edited by Nathaniel Persily, 15–58. New York: Cambridge University Press, 2015.

Barberá, Pablo. "How Social Media Reduces Mass Political Polarization: Evidence from Germany, Spain, and the US." Job Market Paper, New York University, 2014, 1–46.

Bechmann, Anja. "Tackling Disinformation and Infodemics Demands Media Policy Changes." Digital Journalism 8, no. 6 (2020): 855–863. https://doi.org/10.1080/21670811.2020.1773887.

Bennett, W. Lance, and Shanto Iyengar. "A New Era of Minimal Effects? The Changing Foundations of Political Communication." Journal of Communication 58 (2008): 707–731.

Bennett, W. Lance, and Steven Livingston. "The Disinformation Order: Disruptive Communication and the Decline of Democratic Institutions." European Journal of Communication 33, no. 2 (2018): 122–139. https://doi.org/10.1177/0267323118760317.

Bennett, W. Lance, and Steven Livingston. A Brief History of the Disinformation Age: Information Wars and the Decline of Institutional Authority. In Streamlining Political Communication Concepts: Updates, Changes, Normalcies, 43–73. Cham: Springer International Publishing, 2023.

Bennett, W. Lance, and Barbara Pfetsch. "Rethinking Political Communication in a Time of Disrupted Public Spheres." Journal of Communication 68, no. 2 (2018): 243–253. https://doi.org/10.1093/joc/jqx017B.

Bertram, Dane. "Likert Scales... are the meaning of life." (2008). https://www.academia.edu/8160815/Likert_Scales_are_the_meaning_of_life.

Besbris, Max, and Caitlin Petre. "Professionalizing Contingency: How Journalism Schools Adapt to Deprofessionalization." Social Forces 98, no. 4 (2020): 1524–1547. https://doi.org/10.1093/sf/soz094.

Biloš, Antun. "Emerging Focus on Fake News Issues in Scientific Research: A Preliminary Meta-Analysis Approach." Interdisciplinary Management Research 15 (2019): 1139–1150.

Bimber, Bruce, and Homero Gil de Zúñiga. "The Unedited Public Sphere." New Media & Society 22, no. 4 (2022): 700–715.

Bobba, Giuliano. "La Comunicación Política Populista." In Introducción a la Comunicación Política, edited by Gianpietro Mazzoleni, 165–206. Madrid: Alianza Editorial, 2023.

Bovet, Alexandre, and Hernán A. Makse. "Influence of Fake News in Twitter during the 2016 US Presidential Election." Nature Communications 10, no. 1 (2019). https://doi.org/10.1038/s41467-018-07761-2.

Boczkowski, Pablo, and Eugenia Mitchelstein. La Brecha de las Noticias: La Divergencia entre las Preferencias Informativas de los Medios y el Público. Buenos Aires: Manantial, 2015.

Boczkowski, Pablo, Eugenia Mitchelstein, and Mora Matassi. "'News Comes Across When I'm in a Moment of Leisure': Understanding the Practices of Incidental News Consumption on Social Media." New Media & Society 20, no. 10 (2018): 3523–3539. https://doi.org/10.1177/1461444817750396.

Boulianne, Shelley, and Adam Shehata. "Age Differences in Online News Consumption and Online Political Expression in the United States, United Kingdom, and France." The International Journal of Press/Politics 27, no. 3 (2022): 763–783.

References

Bradshaw, Samantha, and Philip N. Howard. "The Global Organization of Social Media Disinformation Campaigns." Journal of International Affairs 71, no. 1.5 (2018): 23–32.

Bruns, Axel. "From 'the' Public Sphere to a Network of Publics: Towards an Empirically Founded Model of Contemporary Public Communication Spaces." Communication Theory 33 (2023): 70–81.

Bustos, Valentín. "Estas Son las Comunidades Autónomas que Lideran las Ocupaciones Ilegales de Inmuebles en 2023." El Español, 21 June 2023. https://www.elespanol.com/invertia/observatorios/vivienda/20230621/comunidades-autonomas-lideran-ocupaciones-ilegales-inmuebles/772922860_0.html.

Cabezas Fernández, María, Ángel Pichel-Vázquez, and Blanca Enguix Grau. "El Marco 'Antigénero' y la (Ultra) Derecha Española: Grupos de Discusión con Votantes de Vox y del Partido Popular." Revista de Estudios Sociales 85 (2023): 97–114.

Callander, Steven, and Juan Carlos Carbajal. "Cause and Effect in Political Polarization: A Dynamic Analysis." Journal of Political Economy 130, no. 4 (2022): 825–880.

Calvo, Dafne, Guillermo López García, and Joaquín Aguar Torres. Periodismo Digital: Ecosistemas, Plataformas y Contenidos. Salamanca: Comunicación Social, 2024.

Carratalá Simón, Adolfo. "Invertir la Vulnerabilidad: El Discurso en Twitter de Organizaciones Neocón y Vox Contra las Personas LGTBI." Quaderns de Filologia. Estudis Lingüístics 26 (2021): 75–94.

Carson, Andrea. Investigative Journalism, Democracy and the Digital Age. London: Routledge, 2019.

Carr, Nicholas. Superficiales: ¿Qué Está Haciendo Internet con Nuestras Mentes? Madrid: Taurus, 2011.

Casal Bértoa, Fernando, and José Rama. "Polarization: What Do We Know and What Can We Do About It?" Frontiers in Political Science 3 (2021): 687695.

Casero-Ripollés, Andreu. "Introducción." In Periodismo y Democracia en el Entorno Digital, edited by Andreu Casero-Ripollés, 11–16. Salamanca: Sociedad Española de Periodística, 2016.

Castells, Manuel. Comunicación y Poder. Madrid: Alianza Editorial, 2009.

Cea, Nereida, and Bella Palomo. "Disinformation Matters: Analyzing the Academic Production." In Politics of Disinformation: The Influence of Fake News on the Public Sphere, 5–22. 2021.

Cervi, Laura, and Andrea Carrillo-Andrade. "Post-Truth and Disinformation: Using Discourse Analysis to Understand the Creation of Emotional and Rival Narratives in Brexit." ComHumanitas: Revista Científica de Comunicación 10, no. 2 (2019): 125–149. https://doi.org/10.31207/rch.v10i2.207.

Chadwick, Andrew. The Hybrid Media System: Politics and Power. New York: Oxford University Press, 2013.

Chen, Hua, and Wing Suen. "Competition for Attention and News Quality." American Economic Journal: Microeconomics 15, no. 3 (2023): 1–32. https://doi.org/10.1257/mic.20210259.

Christians, Clifford G. Normative Theories of the Media: Journalism in Democratic Societies. Urbana: University of Illinois Press, 2009.

CIS, Centro de Investigaciones Sociológicas. "Estudio sobre audiencias de medios de comunicación social." Estudio nº 3421, 2023. https://www.cis.es/documents/d/cis/es3421mar-pdf.

CIS. Estudio no. 3457: Barómetro de Mayo 2024. Accessed May 2024. https://www.cis.es/documents/d/cis/es3457marMT_a.

CIS. Estudio no. 3463: Barómetro de Junio 2024. Accessed June 2024. https://www.cis.es/documents/d/cis/es3463mar_a.

CIS. Estudio no. 3465: Postelectional Elecciones al Parlamento Europeo 2024. Accessed 2024. https://www.cis.es/documents/d/cis/es3465marMT_a.

Cohen, Nicole S. Writers' Rights: Freelance Journalism in a Digital Age. Montreal: McGill-Queen's University Press, 2016.

Cohen, Nicole S., Andrea Hunter, and Penny O'Donnell. "Bearing the Burden of Corporate Restructuring: Job Loss and Precarious Employment in Canadian Journalism." Journalism Practice 13, no. 7 (2019): 817–833. https://doi.org/10.1080/17512786.2019.1571937.

Comisión Europea. "Informe completo Eurobarómetro Estándar 100. Informe Nacional (España)." 2023. https://bit.ly/3KvYGBR.
Corral, David. "Informe Profesión. Periodismo y Sociedad en los Informes APM 2012–2014." Periodistas 37 (2015): 38–41. https://fape.es/wp-content/uploads/2015/04/PDF.pdf.
Costera Meijer, Irene, and Hans P. Bijleveld. "Valuable Journalism: Measuring News Quality from a User's Perspective." Journalism Studies 17, no. 7 (2016): 827–839.
Costera Meijer, Irene. "What is Valuable Journalism? Three Key Experiences and Their Challenges for Journalism Scholars and Practitioners." Digital Journalism 10, no. 2 (2021): 230–252. https://doi.org/10.1080/21670811.2021.1919537.
Crespi, Irving. El Proceso de Opinión Pública. Barcelona: Ariel, 2000.
Cúneo, Martín. "El Fantasma de la Okupación, Agítese Antes de Usar." El Salto, August 28, 2020. https://www.elsaltodiario.com/especulacion-urbanistica/vivienda-desahucio-pah-mentiras-bulos-fantasmaokupacion-agitese-antes-usar.
Curran, James. "The Future of Journalism." Journalism Studies 11, no. 4 (2010): 464–476. https://doi.org/10.1080/14616701003722444.
Dahlgren, Peter. "The Internet, Public Spheres, and Political Communication: Dispersion and Deliberation." Political Communication 22, no. 2 (2005): 147–162.
DESCA (Observatori DESC). 2020. Nou informe sobre l'evolució dels desnonaments 2008–2019 que evidencia que la vulneració del dret a l'habitatge no s'atura. https://observatoridesc.org/ca/nou-informe-sobre-l-evolucio-dels-desnonaments-2008-2019-que-evidencia-que-vulneracio-del-dret-l.
Deuze, Mark. 2005. "What is Journalism? Professional Identity and Ideology of Journalists Reconsidered." Journalism 6 (4): 442–464.
Deuze, Mark, and Tamara Witschge. 2018. "Beyond Journalism: Theorizing the Transformation of Journalism." Journalism 19 (2): 165–181. https://doi.org/10.1177/1464884916688550.
Dias, Nicole, and Alice Sippitt. 2020. "Researching Fact Checking: Present Limitations and Future Opportunities." Political Quarterly 91 (3): 605–613. https://doi.org/10.1111/1467-923X.12892.
Diddi, Arvind, and Robert LaRose. 2006. "Getting Hooked on News: Uses and Gratifications and the Formation of News Habits among College Students in an Internet Environment." Journal of Broadcasting & Electronic Media 50 (2): 193–210.
Diez-Gracia, Alba, and Pilar Sánchez-García. 2022. "Brecha Informativa en la 'Triple Agenda Digital'. Intereses Dispares entre Medio, Audiencia y Redes." Communication & Society 35 (1): 63–80. https://doi.org/10.15581/003.35.1.63-80.
Díez Garrido, Manuel, Cristina Renedo Farpón, and Lorena Cano-Orón. 2021. "La Desinformación en las Redes de Mensajería Instantánea. Estudio de las Fake News en los Canales Relacionados con la Ultraderecha Española en Telegram." Miguel Hernández Communication Journal 12: 467489-467489.
DiMaggio, Paul, John Evans, and Bethany Bryson. 1996. "Have Americans' Social Attitudes Become More Polarized?" American Journal of Sociology 102 (3): 690–755.
Dimmick, John, Yan Chen, and Zhan Li. 2004. "Competition Between the Internet and Traditional News Media: The Gratification-Opportunities Niche Dimension." Journal of Media Economics 17 (1): 19–33.
Doyle, Gillian. 2013. "Re-Invention and Survival: Newspapers in the Era of Digital Multiplatform Delivery." Journal of Media Business Studies 10 (4): 1–20.
Dutta-Bergman, Mohan J. 2004. "Complementarity in Consumption of News Types Across Traditional and New Media." Journal of Broadcasting & Electronic Media 48 (1): 41–60.
Edelman. "Edelman Trust Barometer. Informe España." 2023. https://bit.ly/4camXJj.
EFE. 2024. "¿Cuáles Son las Comunidades que Más Inmigración Reciben?" 14 January 2024. https://efe.com/espana/2024-01-14/comunidades-autonomas-que-mas-inmigracion-reciben/#:~:text=%2D%20Catalu%C3%B1a%2C%20Comunidad%20de%20Madrid%20y,La%20Rioja%2C%20Extremadura%20y%20Cantabria.
EGM, Estudio General de Medios. "Entrega de resultados EGM 3ª ola 2023." 2023.

El País. 2024. "El PP Redobla su Ofensiva Contra los Inmigrantes ante el Temor a Vox: 'Están Aguantando'." 9 May 2024. https://elpais.com/espana/elecciones-catalanas/2024-05-09/el-pp-redobla-su-ofensiva-contra-los-inmigrantes-ante-el-temor-a-vox-estan-aguantando.html.

Ekdale, Brian, Jean B. Singer, Melissa Tully and Shawn Harmsen. "Making change: Diffusion of technological, relational, and cultural innovation in the newsroom." Journalism & mass communication quarterly 92.4 (2015): 938–958.

Escalona, Pablo. 2019. "El Periodismo se Está Convirtiendo en un Mundo de Falsos Autónomos." AyE, 21 January 2019. https://www.autonomosyemprendedor.es/articulo/actualidad/periodismo-convirtiendo-mundo-falsos-autonomos/20190114180354018629.html.

Esser, Frank, and Barbara Pfetsch. "Comparing political communication: A 2020 update." Comparative politics 5 (2020): 336–358.

Eurobarómetro. 2023. Eurobarómetro Standard 100 Otoño 2023. https://spain.representation.ec.europa.eu/document/download/2a1a9875-1f0e-440c-8e9a-48ea9def2e43_es?filename=Informe_EB_100_Oto%C3%B1o_2023.pdf.

European Commission. 2018. A Multi-Dimensional Approach to Disinformation: Report of the Independent High Level Group on Fake News and Online Disinformation. http://bitly.ws/qcbvF.

Europa Press. 2024. "El Congreso Rechaza la Iniciativa de Vox para Expulsar Migrantes Irregulares, con la Abstención del PP." 23 April 2024. https://www.europapress.es/epsocial/migracion/noticia-todos-grupos-congreso-contra-iniciativa-vox-expulsar-migrantes-irregulares-20240423184441.html.

Ferrer-Conill, Raúl. 2016. "Camouflaging Church as State: An Exploratory Study of Journalism's Native Advertising." Journalism Studies 17 (7): 904-914. https://doi.org/10.1080/1461670X.2016.1165138.

FESP (Federación de Sindicatos de Periodistas). 2024. "El Correo de Andalucía Inicia su Nueva Etapa sin Periodistas." 18 February 2024. https://fesperiodistas.org/el-correo-de-andalucia-inicia-su-nueva-etapa-sin-periodistas/

Fletcher, Richard, and Sora Park. "The Impact of Trust in the News Media on Online News Consumption and Participation." Digital Journalism 5, no. 10 (2017): 1281–1299. https://doi.org/10.1080/21670811.2017.1279979.

Franklin, Bob. "The Future of Journalism: In an Age of Digital Media and Economic Uncertainty." Digital Journalism 2, no. 3 (2014): 254–272. https://doi.org/10.1080/21670811.2014.930253.

Freeden, Michael. "Ideologies and political theory: A conceptual approach." Clarendon Press, 1996.

FundéuRAE. "Polarización, Palabra del Año 2023 para la FundéuRAE." FundéuRAE, 2023. https://www.fundeu.es/recomendacion/polarizacion-palabra-del-ano-2023-para-la-fundeurae/.

Funke, Daniel, and Daniela Flamini. "A Guide to Anti-Misinformation Actions Around the World." Poynter Institute, 2024. https://www.poynter.org/ifcn/anti-misinformation-actions/.

García, Amanda. "El PP de Feijóo Radicaliza su Discurso sobre Inmigración en Plena Competición Electoral con Vox." Público, 8 May 2018. https://www.publico.es/politica/pp-feijoo-radicaliza-discurso-inmigracion-plena-competicion-electoral-vox.html.

García de Blas, Elsa. "El PP redobla su ofensiva contra los inmigrantes ante el temor a Vox: 'Están aguantando'". El País, May 9, 2024.

Garrett, R. Kelly, Santiago D. Gvirsman, Benjamin K. Johnson, Yariv Tsfati, Ryan Neo, and Ariel Dal. "Implications of Pro-and Counterattitudinal Information Exposure for Affective Polarization." Human Communication Research 40, no. 3 (2014): 309–332.

Gebremeskel, Getachew G., and Arjen P. de Vries. "The Role of Geographic Information in News Consumption." In Proceedings of the 24th International Conference on World Wide Web, edited by A. Sangemi, S. Leonardi, and A. Panconesi, 755–760. Association for Computing Machinery, 2015.

Gidron, Noam, James Adams, and Will Horne. American Affective Polarization in Comparative Perspective. Cambridge: Cambridge University Press, 2020.

Gil de Zúñiga, Homero, Brian Weeks, and Alberto Ardèvol-Abreu. "Effects of the News-Finds-Me Perception in Communication: Social Media Use Implications for News Seeking and Learning About Politics." Journal of Computer-Mediated Communication 22, no. 3 (2017): 105–123.

Gómez-Mompart, Josep Lluís, Juan Francisco Gutiérrez-Lozano, and Dolors Palau-Sampio (Eds). La Calidad Periodística: Teorías, Investigaciones y Sugerencias Profesionales. Barcelona: Servei de Publicacions de la Universitat Autònoma de Barcelona, Universitat Jaume I, Universitat Pompeu Fabra y Universitat de València, 2013.

Gómez Mompart, Josep Lluís; Palau Sampio, Dolors. "El reto de la excelencia. Indicadores para medir la calidad periodística". En: La calidad periodística. Teorías, investigaciones y sugerencias profesionales. Gómez Mompart, Josep Lluís; Gutiérrez Lozano, Juan Francisco; Palau Sampio, Dolors (Eds.), 17–38. Aldea global, 2013.

Gómez-Mompart, Josep Lluís, Juan Francisco Gutiérrez-Lozano, and Dolors Palau-Sampio. "Los Periodistas Españoles y la Pérdida de la Calidad de la Información: El Juicio Profesional." Comunicar: Revista Científica Iberoamericana de Comunicación y Educación 45, no. 2 (2015): 143–158.

Goyanes, Manuel, and Marta Rodríguez-Castro. "Commercial Pressures in Spanish Newsrooms: Between Love, Struggle and Resistance." Journalism Studies 20, no. 8 (2019): 1088–1109. https://doi.org/10.1080/1461670X.2018.1487801.

Groot Kormelink, Tim, and Irene Costera Meijer. "What Clicks Actually Mean: Exploring Digital News User Practices." Journalism 19, no. 5 (2018): 668–683.

Gutiérrez-Coba, Liliana. "Análisis de la Calidad Informativa, Primer Paso Hacia el Cambio." Palabra Clave 9, no. 1 (2006): 29–56. https://www.redalyc.org/articulo.oa?id=64900102.

Habermas, Jürgen. Historia y Crítica de la Opinión Pública: La Transformación Estructural de la Vida Pública. Barcelona: Gustavo Gili, 1997 [1962].

Habermas, Jürgen. Facticidad y Validez. Madrid: Trotta, 1998.

Habermas, Jürgen. Teoría de la Acción Comunicativa. 2 vols. Madrid: Taurus, 1999.

Habermas, Jürgen. A New Structural Transformation of the Public Sphere and Deliberative Politics. Cambridge: Polity, 2023.

Haller, André, and Kristoffer Holt. "Paradoxical Populism: How PEGIDA Relates to Mainstream and Alternative Media." Information, Communication & Society 22, no. 12 (2019): 1665–1680. https://doi.org/10.1080/1461670X.2018.1487801.

Hanitzsch, Thomas, Jyotika Ramaprasad, Jaime Arroyave, Rosa Berganza, Lieven Hermans, Jan Fredrik Hovden, et al. Worlds of Journalism: Journalistic Cultures Around the Globe. New York: Columbia University Press, 2019.

Hardy, Jonathan. "Commentary: Branded Content and Media-Marketing Convergence." The Political Economy of Communication 5, no. 1 (2017): 81–87. https://bit.ly/3Lkzs7d.

Hetherington, Marc J. "Putting Polarization in Perspective." British Journal of Political Science 39, no. 2 (2009): 413–448.

Herold, Maik, Janine Joachim, Cyrill Otteni, and Hans Vorländer. Polarization in Europe: Quantitative Analysis by Country. MIDEM Study 2024-1. Mercator Forum Migration and Democracy (MIDEM), Dresden, 2024. https://forum-midem.de/wp-content/uploads/2024/02/TUD_MIDEM_Polarisationsstudie_ENG_ES.pdf.

IAB. Estudio Anual de Redes Sociales 2023. https://blog.elogia.net/claves-del-estudio-anual-redes-sociales-2023-iab-spain-by-elogia.

International Labour Organization (ILO). From Precarious Work to Decent Work: Outcome Document to the Workers' Symposium on Policies and Regulations to Combat Precarious Employment. Geneva: ILO, 2012. https://www.ilo.org/wcmsp5/groups/public/%2D%2D-ed_dialogue/%2D%2D-actrav/documents/meetingdocument/wcms_179787.pdf.

InfoAdex. Estudio InfoAdex de la Inversión Publicitaria en España 2007. Madrid: InfoAdex, 2008. https://www.infoadex.es/home/wp-content/uploads/2017/12/RESUMEN-2008.pdf.

InfoAdex. Estudio InfoAdex de la Inversión Publicitaria en España 2023. Madrid: InfoAdex, 2024. https://www.infoadex.es/wp-content/uploads/2024/02/Estudio-InfoAdex-2024-Resumen.pdf.

Invertia. "El Español Pulveriza con 18,6 Millones en Diciembre el Récord de GfK DAM y Ratifica su Liderazgo Absoluto." Invertia, 16 January 2024. https://www.elespanol.com/invertia/medios/20240116/espanol-pulveriza-millones-diciembre-record-gfk-dam-ratifica-liderazgo-absoluto/825167803_0.html#:~:text=E.%20E.

References

Iosifidis, Petros, and Nicholas Nicoli. Digital Democracy, Social Media and Disinformation. London: Routledge, 2020.

Iyengar, Shanto, and Kyu S. Hahn. "Red media, blue media: Evidence of ideological selectivity in media use." Journal of communication 59.1 (2009): 19–39.

Iyengar, Shanto, Gaurav Sood, and Yphtach Lelkes. "Affect, Not Ideology: A Social Identity Perspective on Polarization." Public Opinion Quarterly 76, no. 3 (2012): 405–431.

Jenkins, Henry. Convergence Culture: La Cultura de la Convergencia en los Medios de Comunicación. Barcelona: Paidós, 2008.

Josephi, Beate. "How Much Democracy Does Journalism Need?" Journalism 14, no. 4 (2013): 474–489. https://doi.org/10.1177/1464884912464172.

Jungherr, Andreas, and Ralph Schroeder. "Disinformation and the Structural Transformations of the Public Arena: Addressing the Actual Challenges to Democracy." Social Media + Society 7, no. 1 (2021). https://doi.org/10.1177/2056305121988928.

Kalogeropoulos, Antonis, Jane Suiter, Lukas Udris, and Mark Eisenegger. "News Media Trust and News Consumption: Factors Related to Trust in News in 35 Countries." International Journal of Communication 13 (2019): 3672–3693.

Katz, Elihu, Jay G. Blumler, and Michael Gurevitch. "Utilization of Mass Communication by Individual." In Sources Notable Selections in Mass Media, edited by J. Hanson and D. Maxcy, 51–59. Guilford, CT: Dushkin/McGraw-Hill, 1999.

Katz, Elihu, Jay G. Blumler, and Michael Gurevitch. "Uses and gratifications research." The public opinion quarterly 37.4 (1973): 509–523.

Kaun, Anne, and Emiliano Treré. "Repression, Resistance and Lifestyle: Charting (Dis)connection and Activism in Times of Accelerated Capitalism." Social Movement Studies 19, no. 5-6 (2020): 697–715.

Keller, Bernd, and Hartmut Seifert. "Atypical Employment in Germany: Forms, Development, Patterns." Transfer: European Review of Labour and Research 19, no. 4 (2013): 457–474. https://doi.org/10.1177/1024258913501757.

Killebrew, Kenneth C. Managing Media Convergence: Pathways to Journalistic Cooperation. Ames, IA: Blackwell, 2005.

Klimkiewicz, Beata. Pluralism in a Hybrid Media Environment from the User Perspective. European University Institute, 2019.

Kovach, Bill, and Tom Rosenstiel. The Elements of Journalism. Crown, 2001.

Lacy, Stephen, and Tom Rosenstiel. Defining and Measuring Quality Journalism. New Brunswick, NJ: Rutgers School of Communication and Information, 2015.

Lasswell, Harold D. "The Structure and Function of Communication in Society." In The Communication of Ideas, edited by L. Bryson, 37–51. New York: Institute for Religious and Social Studies, 1948.

Lanier, Jaron. Contra el Rebaño Digital. Barcelona: Random House, 2011.

Lévy, Pierre. Ciberdemocracia: Ensayo Sobre Filosofía Política. Barcelona: Editorial UOC, 2002.

Lewandowsky, Stephan, Ullrich K. H. Ecker, and John Cook "Beyond Misinformation: Understanding and Coping with the 'Post-truth' Era." Journal of Applied Research in Memory and Cognition 6, no. 4 (2017): 353–369. https://doi.org/10.1016/j.jarmac.2017.07.008.

Lippmann, Walter. Public Opinion. New York: The Free Press, 1922.

Llorca-Abad, Germán, and José Gamir-Ríos. "La Sociedad de las Turbas, La Sociedad de la Incomunicación." Inmediaciones de la Comunicación 18, no. 1 (2023): 43–65.

Lockie, Stewart. "Post-truth Politics and the Social Sciences." Environmental Sociology 3, no. 1 (2017): 1–5. https://doi.org/10.1080/23251042.2016.1273444.

López García, Guillermo. Periodismo Digital: Redes, Audiencias y Modelos de Negocio. Salamanca: Comunicación Social, 2015.

López García, Guillermo, and Eva Campos Domínguez, eds. Redes en Campaña: Liderazgos y Mensajes en Las Elecciones de 2019. Salamanca: Comunicación Social, 2021.

López-García, Guillermo, Dolors Palau-Sampio, Bella Palomo, Eva Campos-Domínguez, and Pere Masip, eds. Politics of Disinformation: The Influence of Fake News on the Public Sphere. Hoboken: Wiley Blackwell, 2021.

López García, Guillermo, ed. Ecología de la Desinformación y Su Impacto en El Espacio Público. New York: Peter Lang, 2023.

López-García, Guillermo, and Lidia Valera-Ordaz. "La Esfera Pública Postmediática." Debats 138, no. 1 (2024): 98–114.

Lu, Yiran, and Jayeon Lee. "Partisan Information Sources and Affective Polarization: Panel Analysis of the Mediating Role of Anger and Fear." Journalism & Mass Communication Quarterly 96, no. 3 (2019): 767–783. https://doi.org/10.1177/1077699018811295.

Macnamara, Jim. "The Continuing Convergence of Journalism and PR: New Insights for Ethical Practice from a Three-country Study of Senior Practitioners." Journalism & Mass Communication Quarterly 93, no. 1 (2016): 118–141. https://doi.org/10.1177/1077699015605803.

Malik, Asmaa, and Ivor Shapiro. "What's digital? What's journalism?." The Routledge companion to digital journalism studies. Routledge, 2016. 15–24.

Marcos, José. "El Gobierno Estudia 'Alternativas' Para Renovar El Consejo Del Poder Judicial Sin El PP Tras 2,000 Días de Bloqueo." El País, 26 May 2024. https://elpais.com/espana/2024-05-26/el-gobierno-estudia-alternativas-para-renovar-el-consejo-del-poder-judicial-sin-el-pp-tras-2000-dias-de-bloqueo.html.

Mazzoleni, Gianpietro, and Winfried Schulz. "'Mediatization' of Politics: A Challenge for Democracy?" Political Communication 16, no. 3 (1999): 247–261.

Mazzoleni, Gianpietro. "Mediatization and Political Populism." In Mediatization of Politics: Understanding the Transformation of Western Democracies, edited by Frank Esser and Jesper Strömbäck, 42–57. Basingstoke: Palgrave Macmillan, 2014.

Mazzoleni, Gianpietro, ed. Introducción a La Comunicación Política. Madrid: Alianza Editorial, 2023.

McCombs, Maxwell, and Donald Shaw. "The Agenda Setting Function of the Mass Media." Public Opinion Quarterly 36 (1972): 176–187.

McCoy, Jennifer, Tarek Masoud, and Murat Somer. "Polarization and the Global Crisis of Democracy: Common Patterns, Dynamics, and Pernicious Consequences for Democratic Polities." American Behavioral Scientist 62, no. 1 (2018): 16–42. https://doi.org/10.1177/0002764218759576.

McCoy, Jennifer. "Polarization Harms Democracy and Society." Dialogue in Polarised Societies, June 2019. https://www.icip.cat/perlapau/en/article/polarization-harms-democracy-and-society/?pdf.

McCoy, Jennifer, and Murat Somer. "Toward a Theory of Pernicious Polarization and How It Harms Democracies: Comparative Evidence and Possible Remedies." The Annals of the American Academy of Political and Social Science 681, no. 1 (2019): 234–271.

McKay, Spencer, and Chris Tenove. "Disinformation as a Threat to Deliberative Democracy." Political Research Quarterly 74, no. 3 (2021): 703–717.

McLuhan, Marshall. Comprender los Medios de Comunicación: Las Extensiones del Ser Humano. Barcelona: Paidós, 1996 [1964].

McNair, Brian. "Journalism and Democracy." In The Handbook of Journalism Studies, edited by Karin Wahl-Jorgensen and Thomas Hanitzsch, 237–249. London: Routledge, 2009.

McQuail, Denis. "Mass communication theory: An introduction." Sage Publications, Inc, 1994.

McQuail, Denis. McQuail's Mass Communication Theory. 5th ed. London: Sage, 2005.

McQuail, Denis. McQuail's mass communication theory. Sage, 2012.

Meier, Klaus. "Quality in journalism." The international encyclopedia of journalism studies (2019): 1–8.

Merrill, John C. The Elite Press: Great Newspapers of the World. Pitman, 1968.

Miller, Laura. "La Polarización Política en España: Entre Ideologías y Sentimientos." PAPELES de Relaciones Ecosociales y Cambio Global (152) (2020): 13–22. https://www.fuhem.es/papeles_articulo/la-polarizacion-politica-en-espana-entre-ideologias-y-sentimientos/.

References

Miller, Laura, and Mariano Torcal. "Veinticinco Años de Polarización Afectiva en España." The Conversation, 2020. https://theconversation.com/veinticinco-anos-de-polarizacion-afectiva-en-espana-149237.

Moisander, Johanna, Christina Groß, and Karoliina Eräranta. "Mechanisms of Biopower and Neoliberal Governmentality in Precarious Work: Mobilizing the Dependent Self-Employed as Independent Business Owners." Human Relations 71, no. 3 (2018): 375–398. https://doi.org/10.1177/0018726717718918.

Morozov, Evgeny. El Desengaño de Internet: Los Mitos de la Libertad en la Red. Barcelona: Destino, 2011.

Mudde, Cas. Populist Radical Right Parties in Europe. Cambridge: Cambridge University Press, 2007.

Mudde, Cas, and Cristóbal Rovira Kaltwasser. Populism: A Very Short Introduction. Oxford: Oxford University Press, 2017.

Netanel, N. W. "Mandating Digital Platform Support for Quality Journalism." Harvard Journal of Law & Technology 34 (2020): 473.

Newman, Nic, and Richard Fletcher. "Bias, bullshit and lies: Audience perspectives on low trust in the media." Reuters Institute for the Study of Journalism, 2017.

Newman, Nic, Rasmus Kleis Nielsen, David A. L. Fletcher, Kalina Bontcheva, and Richard Fletcher. Reuters Institute Digital News Report 2022. Reuters Institute, University of Oxford, 2022. https://reutersinstitute.politics.ox.ac.uk/sites/default/files/2022-06/Digital_News-Report_2022.pdf.

Newman, Nic, Rasmus Kleis Nielsen, David A. L. Fletcher, A.R. Arguedas, and Richard Fletcher. Reuters Institute Digital News Report 2024. Reuters Institute for the Study of Journalism, 2024. https://reutersinstitute.politics.ox.ac.uk/sites/default/files/2024-06/RISJ_DNR_2024_Digital_v10%20lr.pdf.

Norbäck, Mattias, and Andreas Styhre. "On the Precarity-Spectrum: Exploring Different Levels of Precariousness in Market-Mediated Professional Work." Management Revue 32, no. 3 (2021): 266–295. https://doi.org/10.5771/0935-9915-2021-3-266.

Olmos Alcaraz, Antonio. "Desinformación, Posverdad, Polarización y Racismo en Twitter: Análisis del Discurso de Vox Sobre las Migraciones Durante la Campaña Electoral Andaluza (2022)." Methaodos.Revista De Ciencias Sociales 11, no. 1 (2023): m231101a09. 10.17502/mrcs.v11i1.676.

Olmos-Alcaraz, Antonio. "Populism and Racism on Social Networks: An Analysis of the Vox Discourse on Twitter During the Ceuta 'Migrant Crisis'." Catalan Journal of Communication & Cultural Studies 14, no. 2 (2022): 207–223.

Örnebring, Henrik. "Journalists Thinking About Precarity: Making Sense of the 'New Normal'." International Symposium on Online Journalism 8, no. 1 (2018): 109–127. https://isoj.org/wp-content/uploads/2018/04/FINALISOJ.pdf.

Örnebring, Henrik, and Cecilia Möller. "In the Margins of Journalism: Gender and Livelihood Among Local (Ex-) Journalists in Sweden." Journalism Practice 12, no. 8 (2018): 1051–1060. https://doi.org/10.1080/17512786.2018.1497455.

Palau-Sampio, Dolors. "Pseudo-Media Sites, Polarization, and Pandemic Skepticism in Spain." Frontiers in Political Science 3 (2021a): 685295.

Palau-Sampio, Dolors. "Sponsored Content in Spanish Media: Strategies, Transparency, and Ethical Concerns." Digital Journalism 9, no. 7 (2021b): 908–928. https://doi.org/10.1080/21670811.2021.1966314.

Palau-Sampio, Dolors, and Adolfo Carratalá. "Injecting Disinformation into Public Space: Pseudo-Media and Reality-Altering Narratives." Profesional de la Información 31, no. 3 (2022).

Palau-Sampio, Dolors, and Guillermo López-García. "Communication and Crisis in the Public Space: Dissolution and Uncertainty." Profesional de la Información 31, no. 3 (2022).

Palau-Sampio, Dolors. "Pseudo-Media Disinformation Patterns: Polarised Discourse, Clickbait and Twisted Journalistic Mimicry." Journalism Practice 17, no. 10 (2023): 2140–2158. https://doi.org/10.1080/17512786.2022.2126992.

Palau-Sampio, Dolors, and Maria Iranzo-Cabrera. "Índice de Calidad del Branded Content Informativo en España: Criterios y Evaluación." Revista de Comunicación 23, no. 1 (2024): 395–412. https://doi.org/10.26441/RC23.1-2024-3390.

Papacharissi, Zizi, and Ariel M. Rubin. "Predictors of Internet Use." Journal of Broadcasting & Electronic Media 44, no. 2 (2000): 175–196.

Pariser, Eli. The Filter Bubble: What the Internet Is Hiding from You. New York: Penguin Press, 2011.

Pellegrini, Silvia, and M. C. Mujica. "Valor Agregado Periodístico (VAP): La Calidad Periodística Como un Factor Productivo en un Entorno Medial Complejo." Palabra Clave 9, no. 1 (2006): 11–28. https://www.redalyc.org/pdf/649/64900101.pdf.

Pellegrini, Silvia, Soledad Puente, William Porath, Constanza Mujica, and Daniela Grassau. La apuesta por la calidad de las noticias Journalistic added Value: the commitment to the quality of news. Ediciones UC, 2011.

Pérez, Francisco, Bruno Broseta, Alejandro Escribá, Guillermo López García, Joaquín Maudos, and Fernando Pascual. Los Medios de Comunicación en la Era Digital. Bilbao: Fundación BBVA, 2023.

Price, Vincent. La Opinión Pública. Barcelona: Paidós, 1994.

Qureshi, Iftikhar, Bharat Bhatt, Shubham Gupta, and A. A. Tiwari. "Causes, Symptoms and Consequences of Social Media Induced Polarization (SMIP)." Information Systems Journal 11 (2020): 1–11.

Ramírez-de-la-Piscina, Txema, Beatriz Zabalondo-Loidi, Antxoka Agirre-Maiora, and Alazne Aiestarán. "La Calidad de la Prensa Europea de Referencia Analizada por Académicos, Profesionales y Usuarios." Estudios sobre el Mensaje Periodístico 21, no. 1 (2015): 31–46. https://doi.org/10.5209/rev_ESMP.2015.v21.50649.

Reiljan, Anu. "Fear and Loathing Across Party Lines (Also) in Europe: Affective Polarisation in European Party Systems." European Journal of Political Research 59, no. 2 (2020): 376–396.

Reinemann, Carsten, James Stanyer, Steffen Scherr, and Gianpietro Legnante. "Hard and Soft News: A Review of Concepts, Operationalizations and Key Findings." Journalism 13, no. 2 (2012): 221–239. https://doi.org/10.1177/1464884911427803.

Rheingold, Howard. Multitudes Inteligentes: La Próxima Revolución Social. Barcelona: Gedisa, 2002.

Rid, Thomas. Active Measures: The Secret History of Disinformation and Political Warfare. New York: Farrar, Straus and Giroux, 2020.

Roncesvalles Labiano-Juangarcía, M. Fernanda Novoa-Jaso, Auken Sierra-Iso, and Alfonso Vara-Miguel. Digital News Report España 2024. https://dadun.unav.edu/handle/10171/69541?_ga=2.213170196.1618751582.1719778131-1123249037.1719068582.

Rúas Araújo, José, and Francisco-Javier Paniagua Rojano. "Aproximación al Mapa sobre la Investigación en Desinformación y Verificación en España: Estado de la Cuestión." ICONO 14. Revista Científica de Comunicación y Tecnologías Emergentes 21, no. 1 (2023).

Ruggiero, Thomas. "Uses and Gratifications Theory in the 21st Century." Mass Communication & Society 3 (2000): 3–37.

Sádaba, C., and R. Salaverría. "Combatir la Desinformación con Alfabetización Mediática: Análisis de las Tendencias en la Unión Europea." Revista Latina de Comunicación Social 81 (2023): 17-33. https://doi.org/10.4185/RLCS-2023-1552.

Salaverría, Ramón; L. Alberto García Avilés, and Pere Masip. "Concepto de convergencia periodística." En X. López García y X. Pereira (Ed.), Convergencia Digital. Reconfiguración de los medios de comunicación en España. Santiago, Universidad de Santiago, Servicio de Publicaciones, 41–64, 2010.

Salaverría, R., N. Buslón, F. López-Pan, B. León, I. López-Goñi, and M. C. Erviti. "Desinformación en Tiempos de Pandemia: Tipología de los Bulos sobre la Covid-19." Profesional de la Información 29, no. 3 (2020).

Sallot, Lynne M., and Elizabeth A. Johnson. "Investigating Relationships Between Journalists and Public Relations Practitioners: Working Together to Set, Frame and Build the Public Agenda,

1991–2004." Public Relations Review 32, no. 2 (2006): 151–159. https://doi.org/10.1016/j.pubrev.2006.02.008.

Sampedro, Víctor. Opinión Pública y Democracia Deliberativa: Medios, Sondeos y Urnas. Madrid: Istmo, 2000.

Sampedro, Víctor. Teorías de la Comunicación y el Poder: Opinión Pública y Pseudocracia. Madrid: Akal, 2023.

Sánchez-Duarte, José Manuel, and Raúl Magallón Rosa. "Infodemia y COVID-19: Evolución y Viralización de Informaciones Falsas en España." Revista Española de Comunicación en Salud (2020): 31–41.

Sani, G., and G. Sartori. "Polarization, Fragmentation and Competition in Western Democracies." In Western European Party Systems, edited by H. Daalder and P. Mair. Beverly Hills: Sage, 1983.

Shao, Chengcheng, Giovanni Luca Ciampaglia, Onur Varol, Alessandro Flammini, and Filippo Menczer. "The Spread of Misinformation by Social Bots." arXiv preprint arXiv:1707.07592 (2017).

Schäfer, Mike. "Digital Public Sphere." In The International Encyclopaedia of Political Communication, edited by Gianpietro Mazzoleni et al., 322–328. London: Wiley Blackwell, 2015.

Scheufele, Dietram A., and Norbert M. Krause. "Science Audiences, Misinformation, and Fake News." Proceedings of the National Academy of Sciences 116, no. 16 (2019): 7662–7669. https://www.pnas.org/content/116/16/7662.

Schia, N. N., and L. Gjesvik. "Hacking Democracy: Managing Influence Campaigns and Disinformation in the Digital Age." Journal of Cyber Policy 5, no. 3 (2020): 413-428.

Schibsted. "Users' Trust in Editorial Media Is Influenced by Four Key Drivers." 30 April 2024. https://schibsted.com/news/users-trust-in-editorial-media-is-influenced-by-four-key-drivers/.

Schlesinger, Philip. "After the Post-Public Sphere." Media, Culture & Society 42, no. 7 (2020): 1545–1563.

Schudson, Michael. Why Democracies Need an Unlovable Press. Cambridge: Polity, 2008.

Schudson, Michael. "How to Think Normatively about News and Democracy." In The Oxford Handbook of Political Communication, edited by Kate Kenski and Katherine H. Jamieson. Oxford: Oxford University Press, 2015. https://doi.org/10.1093/oxfordhb/9780199793471.013.73.

Schulz, Winfried. "Reconstructing Mediatization as an Analytical Concept." European Journal of Communication 19 (2004): 87–101.

Schulz, Winfried. Preconditions of Journalistic Quality in an Open Society. Proceedings of International Conference "News Media and Politics – Independent Journalism", Budapest, 6–7 October. 2000.

Schünemann, W. J. "A Threat to Democracies?: An Overview of Theoretical Approaches and Empirical Measurements for Studying the Effects of Disinformation." Cyber Security Politics (2022): 32–47.

Shoemaker, Pamela J., J. H. Lee, G. Han, and A. A. Cohen. "Proximity and Scope as News Values." In Media Studies: Key Issues and Debates, edited by E. Devereux, 231–248. London: SAGE Publications, 2007.

Shu, Kai, A. Bhattacharjee, F. Alatawi, T. H. Nazer, K. Ding, M. Karami, and H. Liu. "Combating Disinformation in a Social Media Age." Wiley Interdisciplinary Reviews: Data Mining and Knowledge Discovery 10, no. 6 (2020): e1385.

Simón, Pedro. "The Multiple Spanish Elections of April and May 2019: The Impact of Territorial and Left-Right Polarisation." South European Society and Politics 25, no. 3–4 (2020): 441–474. https://doi.org/10.1080/13608746.2020.1756612.

Siwakoti, Sudhir, Kiran Yadav, Nydia Bariletto, Luca Zanotti, Ugur Erdogdu, and Jonathan N. Shapiro. "How COVID Drove the Evolution of Fact-Checking." Harvard Kennedy School Misinformation Review (2021).

Spurk, Christoph. "Measuring Quality in Journalism: How and What For?" In Entrepreneurial Journalism in Africa: Opportunities, Challenges and Risks for Media in the Digital Age, edited by Francis Mdlongwa, 28–31. Johannesburg: Konrad-Adenauer-Stiftung, 2019. https://bit.ly/3wvFXyI.

Stencel, Matt, Emily Ryan, and Joshua Luther. "Misinformation Spreads, but Fact-Checking Has Leveled Off." Duke Reporters' Lab, 21 June 2023. https://reporterslab.org/misinformation-spreads-but-fact-checking-has-leveled-off/. Accessed 28 September 2023

Strömbäck, Jesper, Mikael Djerf-Pierre, and Anders Shehata. "The Dynamics of Political Interest and News Media Consumption: A Longitudinal Perspective." International Journal of Public Opinion Research 25, no. 4 (2013): 414–435.

Stroud, N. J. "Polarization and Partisan Selective Exposure." Journal of Communication 60, no. 3 (2010): 556–576. https://doi.org/10.1111/j.1460-2466.2010.01497.x.

Sunstein, Cass. República.com: Internet, Democracia y Libertad. Barcelona: Paidós, 2003.

Sunstein, Cass. How Change Happens. Cambridge: MIT Press, 2019.

Svolik, Milan W. "Polarization versus Democracy." Journal of Democracy 30 (2019): 20.

Sundar, S. Shyam. "Exploring Receivers' Criteria for Perception of Print and Online News." Journalism & Mass Communication Educator 76 (1999): 373–386.

Sybert, J. "Navigating Precarity: Disruption and Decline at the Pittsburgh Post-Gazette." Journalism Practice 17, no. 4 (2023): 737–754. https://doi.org/10.1080/17512786.2021.1939105.

Taguieff, Pierre-André. L'Illusion Populiste: De l'Archaïque au Médiatique. Paris: Berg International, 2002.

Tenove, Claire. "Protecting Democracy from Disinformation: Normative Threats and Policy Responses." The International Journal of Press/Politics 25, no. 3 (2020): 517–537.

The Trust Project. "About Us." Accessed 6 September 2024. https://thetrustproject.org/about/.

The Trust Project. "Learn the 8 Trust Indicators." Accessed 6 September 2024. https://thetrustproject.org/Trusted-Journalism/.

Torcal, Mariano, and José Manuel Comellas. "Affective Polarisation in Times of Political Instability and Conflict: Spain from a Comparative Perspective." South European Society and Politics 27, no. 1 (2022): 1–26. https://doi.org/10.1080/13608746.2022.2044236.

Tsfati, Yariv. "Online News Exposure and Trust in the Mainstream Media: Exploring Possible Associations." American Behavioral Scientist 54, no. 1 (2010): 22–42.

Tucker, Joshua Aaron, Andrew Guess, Pablo Barbera, Cristian Vaccari, Alexandra Siegel, Sergey Sanovich, Denis Stukal, and Brendan Nyhan. "Social Media, Political Polarization, and Political Disinformation: A Review of the Scientific Literature." March 19, 2018. Available at SSRN: https://ssrn.com/abstract=3144139 or https://doi.org/10.2139/ssrn.3144139.

United Nations (UN). "Countering Disinformation." Accessed 6 Sept 2024. https://www.un.org/en/countering-disinformation.

Van der Wurff, R. "Are News Media Substitutes? Gratifications, Contents, and Uses." Journal of Media Economics 24, no. 3 (2011): 139–157. https://doi.org/10.1080/08997764.2011.601974.

Van Der Wurff, R., and K. Schoenbach. "Civic and Citizen Demands of News Media and Journalists: What Does the Audience Expect from Good Journalism?" Journalism & Mass Communication Quarterly 91, no. 3 (2014): 433–451.

Van Prooijen, Jan Willem, A. Peter Krouwel, and Thomas V. Pollet. "Political Extremism Predicts Belief in Conspiracy Theories." Social Psychological and Personality Science 6, no. 5 (2015): 570–578.

Van Raemdonck, Nele, and Tine Meyer. "Why Disinformation Is Here to Stay: A Socio-technical Analysis of Disinformation as a Hybrid Threat." In Addressing Hybrid Threats: European Law and Policies, edited by Luca Lonardo, 57–83. Cheltenham: Edward Elgar, 2024. https://cris.vub.be/ws/portalfiles/portal/82250992/Van_Raemdonck_Meyer_Hybrid_Threats_of_Disinformation.pdf.

Vehkoo, J. "What Is Quality Journalism and How It Can Be Saved." Reuters Institute for the Study of Journalism, 2010. https://bit.ly/3x5dggp.

Viner, Katherine. "A Mission for Journalism in a Time of Crisis." The Guardian, 6 November 2017. https://www.theguardian.com/news/2017/nov/16/a-mission-for-journalism-in-a-time-of-crisis.

Waisbord, Silvio. "The Elective Affinity Between Post-Truth Communication and Populist Politics." Communication Research and Practice 4, no. 1 (2018): 17–34. https://doi.org/10.1080/22041451.2018.1428928.

Waisbord, Silvio. "¿Es Válido Atribuir la Polarización Política a la Comunicación Digital? Sobre Burbujas, Plataformas y Polarización Afectiva." Revista SAAP 14, no. 2 (2020): 248–279. https://doi.org/10.46468/rsaap.14.2.a1.

Walker, Megan. "U.S. Newsroom Employment Has Fallen 26% Since 2008." Pew Research Center, 13 July 2021. https://www.pewresearch.org/short-reads/2021/07/13/u-s-newsroom-employment-has-fallen-26-since-2008/.

Wardle, Claire, and Hossein Derakhshan. Information Disorder: Toward an Interdisciplinary Framework for Research and Policy Making. Council of Europe report DGI, September 2017. https://rm.coe.int/information-disorderreportnovember-2017/1680764666.

Wardle, Claire, and Hossein Derakhshan. "Thinking About 'Information Disorder': Formats of Misinformation, Disinformation, and Mal-information." In Journalism, 'Fake News' & Disinformation, edited by Claire Wardle and Hossein Derakhshan, 43–54. Paris: UNESCO, 2018.

Westwood, Peter. Inclusive and adaptive teaching: Meeting the challenge of diversity in the classroom. Routledge, 2018.

Witschge, Tamara, and Göran Nygren. "Journalistic Work: A Profession Under Pressure?" Journal of Media Business Studies 6, no. 1 (2009): 37–59. https://doi.org/10.1080/16522354.2009.11073478.

Wolton, Dominique. Elogio del Gran Público. Barcelona: Gedisa, 1992.

Wolton, Dominique. Internet ¿Y Después? Barcelona: Gedisa, 2000.

Zaller, John. The Nature and Origins of Mass Opinion. New York: Cambridge University Press, 1992.

Zárate, Pedro. "Las Audiencias de 2023: Antena 3 Revalida Su Corona, Telecinco Vive Su Peor Año y La 1 Acapara Las Emisiones Más Vistas." 28 December 2023. https://go.uv.es/b2o0vME.

Zarocostas, John. "How to Fight an Infodemic." The Lancet 395, no. 10225 (2020): 676. https://doi.org/10.1016/s0140-6736(20)30461-x.

The manufacturer's authorised representative in the EU is Springer Nature Customer Service Centre GmbH, Europaplatz 3, 69115 Heidelberg, Germany. If you have any concerns regarding our products, please contact ProductSafety@springernature.com

Printed and bound by CPI Group (UK) Ltd, Croydon, CR0 4YY

23/03/2026

02076360-0009